High on Life

a story of addiction and recovery

by

Lee M. Silverstein, M.S.W.
Jerry Edelwich, M.S.W.
Donald Flanagan

With Narration and Commentary by Archie Brodsky

February 1981

HEALTH COMMUNICATIONS, INC.
2119-A Hollywood Boulevard
Hollywood, Florida 33020

Table of Contents

Published by Health Communications, Inc.
2119-A Hollywood Blvd., Hollywood, Florida 33020

ISBN 0-932194-08-7

"In the midst of darkness
Light persists."
Mr. Gandhi said —
I'm beginning to
See that pinpoint
Of light after
Sometime in darkness —

And it all comes clear —
I don't have to be a
sun
  or a moon
    or a planet
Not even a star —
Not even a flashlight!

Just can be —
That's enough
And being — perhaps
I can shine enough
To light my own way
And perhaps —
For a moment —
Yours —

— *Gene K. Hoffman*, ***From Inside the Glass Doors.***
Brooklyn; The Turning Press, 1977.

acknowledgments

From Lee: Thanks to my sister Barbara and John Cassidy, who started me on the road to life. With love to Leslie, Jon and Amy who will not forget but are beginning to understand.

From Jerry: Thanks to my mother, Tania Edelwich, my sister, Sonia Sadicario, and my brother-in-law, Nathan Sadicario.

From Don: Thanks to Dr. Donald Pet, Carol, Lois, Sandy, Charles Rodgers, Terry Capshaw, my mother, Florence Hawksworth, and the people I'm working with now.

Lee, Jerry, Don and Archie would like to thank our editor Milan Korcok, Stanton Peele, Stephen Merriman, Diana Preice and Pamela Silverstein for their critical reading of parts of the book. We are also grateful to Joanne Sullivan, Donna Gertler, and Amy Meterparel for all their work on the manuscript.

1

introduction

In this book three men share their experiences of addiction and recovery. Lee Silverstein was born in 1930, Jerry Edelwich in 1935, Donald Flanagan in 1940 — a time when every boy was supposed to have a mother and father like Andy Hardy's. They grew up in a world of World War II heroics and Hollywood strongmen — Humphrey Bogart, Edward G. Robinson, John Garfield, John Wayne. Unable to live up to these models except in fantasy, they wandered through an extended adolescence chasing drugs or alcohol "highs," as others then and now have chased the "highs" of addictive work and addictive pleasure. In 1970, then in the early stages of recovery, they met as counselors at the Blue Hills Hospital drug and alcohol rehabilitation clinic in Hartford, Connecticut. Beginning then, and continuing in later years after they had gone their separate ways, they sat down with a tape recorder to make sense of their lives. "Who are we now?" "Who were we then?" "How did we get from the one place to the other?" Those were the questions they posed for themselves, for each other, and for others who might learn from their example.

My own involvement as narrator and analyst grew out of the publication in 1975 of *Love and Addiction*[1], which I co-authored with social psychologist Stanton Peele. A keen observer and interpreter of both "hard " and "soft" data about human behavior, Stanton was convinced that addiction is not, as has been generally assumed, a simple matter of an automatic chemical reaction. In fact, as he has shown, the physiological component of addiction is just the tip of a large and complex iceberg.[2] In *Love and Addiction* Stanton and I presented a comprehensive theory of addiction as an experience. Our argument was that addiction, chemical or non-chemical, can best be understood by looking at the way people feel about themselves — and about the power of drugs or other addictive objects — on the basis of personal history and social influences. Starting from a reinterpretation of narcotic and alcohol addiction, we showed that essentially the same experience occurs with a wide range of addictions, including some clinging love relationships.

With interpersonal (love) addiction Stanton and I were able to make use of original case material in support of our theory. With drug addictions, on the other hand, we developed our case by bringing together a considerable amount of recent research and observation that cast doubt on the inevitability of addiction for those who use opiates. These sources included Isidor Chein's studies of ghetto heroin addicts in New York, Norman Zinberg's reports on hospital patients' reactions to morphine, Lee Robins' followup surveys of Vietnam veterans who had used heroin during the war, and Charles Winick's analysis of the "maturing out" phenomenon. Together they made a convincing case. What we lacked, though, was first hand testimony from people who have been addicted to narcotics or alcohol.

That is what Lee, Jerry, and Don have provided with their taped reminiscences. Stanton and I had contended that addiction is an experience; these tapes contain several lifetimes worth of experience. Lee, Jerry and Don are saying what *Love and Addiction* says: that it is not the addictive substance that matters, but the feelings that lead to addiction, feelings that are shared by many who do not abuse drugs or alcohol. What matters is not the choice of escape, but the choice *to* escape. Thus, the three men's accounts raise questions that go far beyond drug and alcohol addiction to the basic issues that everyone faces in life.

3

How do human beings cope with pain? What makes some people choose to get high on drugs while others choose to get high on life? How do people change — how *can* people change — from one method of coping, one set of "living skills," to another? What do the singularly dramatic life histories of the alcoholic and the drug addict have to say about the cigarette smoker, the overeater, the workaholic, the gambler, the person who gets involved in compulsive sexuality or destructive love relationships?

***

Where did Lee, Jerry, and Don come from, and where are they now?

Lee Silverstein grew up with all the advantages except the ones that really matter — peace of mind and a sense of belonging. These he tried to find in alcohol and barbiturates. Following in the footsteps of a hard-driving father, Lee went from the Harvard Business School to extraordinary successes in the insurance business, but he remained as unforgiving of himself as he felt his father to be.

Born of a broken family in the Bronx, Jerry Edelwich grew up without benefit of home or school. A child of the streets, he gave himself, in his words, "options that eleven and twelve-year-olds don't have!" In his upside-down Jewish community, the way to achieve success was to be the best dope hustler and the best second-story man on the block. Like the respectable executive who works twelve-hour days to avoid the feeling of being alone (and seeks respite in alcohol), Jerry lived the driven life of a big-time heroin dealer (and sought respite by shooting up).

Don Flanagan, who like Lee grew up in the Hartford area, was brought up by a loving mother who had to work to support herself and her son. Don never made it through high school; learning for him took place out on the street among friends who eventually introduced him to heroin. Once he found his "high," Don traced and retraced a circular path from the street to prison to hospital and back out again.

Lee took his last drink on October 15, 1969. A few months later Jerry got out of prison, had one last "high," and left the

Bronx for good. As novice counselors at Blue Hills Lee and Jerry met Don, who had become a counselor after entering the methadone program as its first patient in 1967. Today, more than a decade later:

Lee is an inspiration to people all over the country and, increasingly, in other parts of the world. Having learned in Alcoholics Anonymous to identify with other alcoholics whose backgrounds were different but whose feelings were much like his own, he has broadened his vision so as to be able to help people who are not alcoholics or drug abusers, but who still feel the pain of loneliness, anxiety, and inadequacy. After taking his M.S.W. degree and becoming a certified Reality Therapist and Rational-Emotive Therapist, Lee went on to head the alcoholism and human services programs at two Hartford area hospitals (all the while remaining active in A.A.). He is the author of *Consider the Alternative,*[3] an accessible yet inspiring introduction to the self-help and counseling methods associated with Reality Therapy, Rational-Emotive Therapy, Values Clarification, and other humanistic approaches. At human potential workshops, seminars, and conferences, Lee conveys a message of universal hope:

> People seek three things: the ability to solve problems (competence), the ability to entertain themselves (joy), and the ability to get along with other people (relatedness). When people have difficulty in any of these areas, they choose some external solution that seems to bring relief. So let's stop talking about the drugs and other things that people get addicted to, and let's start replacing the skills that support addiction with living skills that make addiction unnecessary.

This is the message of *Consider the Alternative* and of *Love and Addiction* as well.

Jerry, too, is now an M.S.W. and a certified Reality Therapist, but his growth, while just as remarkable, has been in different directions from Lee's. The author (with myself) of *Burnout:*

Stages of Disillusionment in the Helping Professions[4] as well as an upcoming book on sexual dynamics in the client-counselor relationship, Jerry has lived out the lessons learned in his pioneering work on staff burnout. "Take courses; read new books; learn new skills; get more credentials; don't get stuck in a small world," he tells his students and trainees, and indeed, Jerry himself is never to be found standing still. In a given week he may bring his professionalism, compassion, and humor to a university classroom, an old age home, a military installation, and a school for the mentally retarded. The next week he may travel to another part of the country to lead a series of workshops on burnout or human sexuality. Jerry has made a career of teaching, career counseling, and consulting in fields ranging from substance abuse to child abuse. His special contribution to this book is his emphasis on the pitfalls of the recovery career and on the crucial issue of sustained growth versus stagnation for the recovering person.

Sadly Don's life has come to dramatize the very questions that Jerry raises. All three men have known defeats as well as triumphs during their post-addiction careers, but the losses that Don has suffered have compromised his recovery. Having remained a rehabilitation counselor at Blue Hills (without qualifying himself as a professional) for a long and increasingly frustrating decade, Don "burned out" just as the taping sessions for this book were nearing completion. Since losing his job he has lived quietly, depending on the support of family, friends, and a variety of psychotropic medications obtained from physicians. Although he has not returned to the street life (which would be extremely difficult for a man of forty), he is still on methadone. As this book goes to press, he is beginning to use his long involvement with methadone as a springboard for social action. He is working with public agencies in an effort to have methadone distribution procedures better serve the needs of recipients.

These developments have raised some unsettling questions that were not anticipated when this book was first conceived. Is it possible to tell when a person has recovered from an addiction? How was it that Don's new life no longer offered him enough comfort and satisfaction to keep him from returning to the old? What light do Don's current difficulties shed on Lee's and Jerry's careers, and vice versa? What things change in a person's life during recovery, and what things remain the same?

These questions are taken up, by Don as well as by Lee and Jerry, in the concluding chapters of the book. Understandably, Don has only begun to be able to talk about the pain that once again is very much in the present for him. In retrospect it seems clear that he never has been able to distance himself securely from the pain that cast a shadow over his early years. From the outset he has not been comfortable with the task of taping his reminiscences (in the early stages of the project he would sometimes take the machine home and work in solitude). It is, therefore, with considerable courage that he has contributed to this book.

To finish a book is simply to reach a more or less arbitrary, more or less appropriate cutoff point. If Lee, Jerry and Don had brought their stories to a close in 1970, or 1974, or 1977, they undoubtedly would have ended on a very different note. Several years ago, for example, they might have concluded that their salvation had come through their work as addiction counselors — a field with which they are no longer so closely involved. Likewise, there is reason to hope that Don's present situation, like other moments of discouragement that are recorded in these pages, will be a beginning rather than an end. For Don, for Lee, for Jerry, for all who must choose between coping by escape and coping by living, the story will go on.

***

To give shape and coherence to the story, I have told it in my own words, with passages from the three men's recollections and reflections liberally interspersed. My analytical commentary is derived from *Love and Addiction* as well as from perspectives that Lee, Jerry and Don have developed and articulated in the course of their lives and work. What I cannot directly convey is the atmosphere of the taping sessions themselves. I can only suggest the verbal electricity generated by these three bearded men, now ranging in age from forty to fifty, all of them seasoned veterans of interpersonal encounters (whether on the street, in prison, in hospitals and clinics, in picaresque personal and sexual adventures, or in family life). Nor can I adequately convey their distinctive speaking styles and mannerisms: Lee's soft, coaxing tone, beneath which lay his considerable drive, insight, and personal force; Jerry's emphatic articulation and elaborate emphases, bespeaking the triumph of his intellectual strength over his early disadvantages; Don's deep bass voice and his manic rambling which, when it was untangled on paper, made beautiful sense.

These, then, are their stories of despair and hope — images of what addiction and recovery *feel* like. Beginning with the deepening spiral of addiction, each man tells in his own way about the fear and the hopelessness, the evasions and manipulations, the delusions and deceptions, the alienation from others, the cycle of self-defeat. Then comes the miracle of recovery — the surrender, the moment of readiness which is not a single moment, but a succession of moments in which a person learns to see himself and his world in a fundamentally different way. What follows is the continuing struggle that anyone faces who is caught between unrealizable goals and hopeless self-doubt — the struggle of learning to live in a world of imperfect but reasonable satisfactions. This is the world Lee and Jerry live in, and those who identify with Don's defeats can find hope in the knowledge that Lee and Jerry, too, have suffered defeats. With their diverse backgrounds, their different accommodations to reality, and the question marks that still punctuate their lives, Lee, Jerry, and Don offer three mirrors for one's own experience, three models for finding one's own truths.

— A.B.

1
beginnings

On the morning of October 15, 1969, in the rooftop restaurant of a Holiday Inn, Lee Silverstein waited for a man with whom he had arranged a business meeting. Lee had arranged many such meetings in his years of wheeling and dealing, but this one was different. This time he was waiting for an angel of death, a representative of organized crime. Lee was about to pay $5000 for the privilege of having himself run off the road by professional killers.

Lee stood by a window that gave restaurant patrons a panoramic view of an old, bleak New England city. In the glass he could see a faint reflection of himself: thirty-nine years old, shabby, unshaven, shaking, retching, hung over. He looked out; it was a long way down. He thought of all the hotels, all the windows from which he had had the impulse to jump.

He had been waiting for death for a long time — weeks, months, years? His business was going under. His marriage had long ago sunk into apathy. Drinking had long since ceased to be fun; he couldn't even drink enough to get drunk anymore. Life had become a succession of blackouts. Each day was the same as every other day: guilt from the night before, anxiety about the night to come. All that was left was to have his debts paid and his family provided for. His insurance policy would pay double indemnity on a murder that was really a suicide made to look like an accident.

How did Lee come to be at that restaurant on that day? How did he bring himself to the point of choosing death? How did Don Flanagan and Jerry Edelwich bring themselves to the point of throwing away their lives in prison?

***

"The issue is not the drug," says Jerry Edelwich, "but the relationship an individual has with the drug, which follows the pattern of other relationships in the individual's life." A person who is addicted to a drug — or to sex, love, work, or eating — is a person whose relationships with people, with work, and with pleasure are lacking in integrity and satisfaction. Addictions come from bad relationships; good relationships are an antidote.

When we hear the word "relationship," we think first of our connections with other people — the earliest and most important kind of relationship we have. All of us sometimes feel alone. To a greater or lesser degree, our loving relationships with others get us through those moments. We choose addictive, self-destructive substitutes to the extent that our relationships are not adequate to support us. A person who chooses a severely debilitating, life-consuming addiction (of which drugs and alcohol are the most visible, though not the only examples) is usually one who feels very much alone.

Images of aloneness run through Lee's, Don's and Jerry's accounts of their early lives. At least in the first two cases they are also images of pain. In Lee's case there is the image of a Jewish kid at Christmas time in the Yankee town of Manchester, Connecticut:

> Christmas was the most awful time for me as a kid. That was the holiday I *wanted* to celebrate. All my friends had trees, and I didn't. The worst thing was that my parents didn't really celebrate Hanukkah either. To them it was just another day; they felt they didn't have to do anything special because they were good parents all year round.

> So at Christmas I would be like a kid pressing his nose against the window. I felt so lonely and out of place and inadequate. In later years that sick, sad feeling would always come back to me at Christmas, and that led to the extravagant "celebrating" I did when I was drinking.

Over in East Hartford, meanwhile, Don was the odd man out among the "tough guys" in the neighborhood gangs:

> I grew up on the street, and the kids there did cruel things like going downtown to roll drunks. I had to show that I was tough enough to hang in and do it, too, but it hurt. I wondered how a guy could eat pie and cookies after clubbing somebody and taking his wallet — and I wondered why it bothered me so much. I wanted to be tough like the others, but I seemed to have these extra sensitivities that the others didn't. I couldn't live up to the image of the neighborhood. When I went to bed I'd lie awake thinking about that. That was part of the pain.

For Jerry, hiding out in the interstices of a Jewish community in the Bronx, getting through childhood was a matter of "living by my wits":

> I was very conscious of being at a disadvantage because I couldn't read, and it would grate on me. The radio, the movies — that's where all my education came from. Riding the New York subways when I was thirteen or fourteen, I had to count the stations to know where to get off. To get down to Lexington Avenue, for instance, I got on the Pelham Bay local and counted fourteen stops going and fourteen coming back. By the time I was fifteen I was running errands for the neighborhood bookies. I may not have able to read, but I

> could sure count.

Characteristically, Jerry speaks of "disadvantage" rather than pain. His image of his youth is not one of emotional trauma, but of a scrambling resourcefulness that made up for his not having an education or even a home.

Behind these images were three young lives that were, so to speak, full of emptiness — emptiness, loneliness, and discontent. Lee was the only one of the three who had an outwardly normal family situation — or, as he tells it, "an overprotected Jewish childhood in a tightly disciplined home. The rules were very strict, and somehow I was the one that was always breaking them." Lee's father, an ambitious businessman on his way to becoming a corporation president, was away traveling "about ninety percent of the time." The father that Lee saw the other ten percent of the time was an angry man who gave him "discipline with a belt." Lee, associating his father's violent temper with alcohol, swore he would never take a drink in his life. As he describes the atmosphere in his home,

> I grew up in a house of anger. Most of what I saw and heard was yelling, shouting, fighting. Like a lot of people, I had no one to teach me sensitivity or awareness. I never saw that there was an alternative, another way of getting along — except to seek peace at any price. I dreaded rejection and couldn't bear to be disliked, so I never put up a fight about anything. I ran from every fight as a kid.

And there were fights, for two things set Lee apart visibly from his peers. One was the facial paralysis he was born with, which his father was always trying to get "fixed" by an expensive doctor. The other was his being one of the few Jewish children in the upper- and middle-class Protestant world of Manchester, Connecticut.

Don and Jerry didn't even have the outward stability and respectability that masked Lee's inner misery. Don, living in a crowded government housing project in East Hartford, shuttled between two very different worlds — an idyllic, syrupy home life in which a doting mother and grandmother attended to this every need, and an anarchic street life where he picked up the survival skills that served him so well later. School was not highly valued in either of these settings, and so it didn't mean much to Don, although he stuck it out until he was sixteen.

Jerry did a lot of shuttling, too, among several different worlds in a childhood that was even more colorful and bizarre than Don's. When Jerry speaks of his life he speaks not in the "I" of psychology as Lee and Don do, but in the "we" of sociology. The "we" extends outward from his immediate family to his omnipresent uncles and cousins to his insulated Jewish neighborhood in the Bronx in the 1940's. Looking back, Jerry says, "I didn't know anyone who wasn't Jewish."

Jerry's parents, who met after his mother had already given birth to a daughter, may or may not ever have been married. They lived on Home Relief, the thirties' equivalent of welfare. When America entered the war in 1941 the cloud of proverty that hung over the family lifted as Jerry's father went into the tire business. A year or two later, when Jerry was seven or eight, his parents split up, with his father returning only for infrequent visits.

Jerry, meanwhile, was a terror both at home and in school. He acted up whenever he didn't get his own way, and he terrorized his mother by "bursting into her bedroom when she was with her boyfriend and making a scene." To the extent that he understands his youthful behavior at all, Jerry attributes his waywardness not to the absence of a father, which he claims he shrugged off, but to his kinship with his mother:

> There was a bond between Mom and me (and to some extent my half-sister as well) in opposition to the rest of the family. I inherited a certain untameable quality she had, along with her position as the black sheep of the family. She didn't accept the idea that she had to sacrifice herself for her children the way everybody else did. She was out for her own good time, and

> naturally her brothers and sisters came down on her for it. My cousins extended that attitude to me — just tolerating me, looking down on me — while I took my mother's side and felt alienated from them. I, too, couldn't stand restraints. I can't remember when I wasn't independent. My mother was fun-loving and gregarious, and in those things, too, she was a model for me.

There were also differences between them. Jerry's mother gambled compulsively all her life. Not Jerry. "I, prompted by a strong concern for safety and survival, have always been more conservative." Whereas his mother "not only had a nimble mind, but was attractive and charming and had a lot of admirers," Jerry as a child was very short, was considered homely, and did not know how smart he was. "My mother was the life of the party. I had no such assets as she did, and I felt I had to get along on my own, by my wits."

When Jerry says "on my own," he means it in a way that few American children and very few American Jewish children could even imagine. His mother, who felt that she couldn't handle this difficult child and still have room to live her own life, (in Jerry's words) "optioned me out" first to relatives, who also couldn't cope with him, and then to the Jewish Shelter for Children in Peekskill, New York. Here has was beaten more than he was taught. He did not learn to read and write at Peekskill any more than he had in the year or so that he had spent in public school.

Jerry repeatedly ran away from Peekskill as he had run away from other homes and schools.

> I would always blend back into the neighborhood, which was still strongly ethnic and mutually protective. World War II was ending, the veterans were returning, and "social clubs" for teenagers and young adults were springing up in cellar or loft apartments on almost every block. These were somewhere in between fraternities and street gangs. I had no trouble getting to live in one

> of these social clubs as a sort of adopted pet — a role which I enjoyed. It didn't matter whose child I was, where I came from, or if anyone knew me. I was a child from the neighborhood, and if I needed care, I was cared for. Club members and their parents brought in food and clothing for me.
>
> The neighborhood was my world, and I was comfortable in it. It consisted of about twenty square blocks, and it was very insular and self-contained. There were neighborhoods much like it on the East Side as well as in Brooklyn. During the war no one had a car, but you didn't need one. There were no shopping centers; everything you needed was in the neighborhood. Stores, movies, the synagogue — everything was right here. To this day those twenty square blocks give me a feeling that I get nowhere else.

In this ethnic milieu Jerry with some relish "went about the business of surviving." He spent his days shoplifting and hanging out at the corner candy store, the poolroom, and the neighborhood movie house.

> All that time I understood that my mother was looking for me, but evidently she wasn't looking too hard, because she never found me. There were times when I was picked up and sent back to Peekskill. But mostly I just took off on my own. Now I realize that I gave myself options that eleven- and twelve-year-olds don't have!

***

Lee has said to Don, "In listening to you I can't get over the way we had the same fears, the same thoughts, the same hassles. With all the differences in our backgrounds, we were facing fundamentally the same thing." When Jerry speaks of having given himself "options that eleven- and twelve-year-olds don't have," he could be speaking for all three men. They all gave themselves options other kids didn't have because they felt that they hadn't been given options other kids have, particularly the option of a reasonably happy life with a nurturant, supportive family.

It is, of course, questionable how many people ever have this option. Many of the children whom Lee, Don and Jerry envied may have been less happy with their secure home lives than was apparent to an "outsider." Some of them may have been headed for addictions, too — perhaps more socially acceptable addictions than Lee's, Don's or Jerry's. Still, it is clear that Lee, Don, and Jerry were not happy and that they suffered from severe dislocations in their family and social relationships. In each case there was a strong feeling of isolation, discomfort, and lack of acceptance in the home and the community. Don speaks for all three when he says, "It was a matter of being alone, of not belonging, of not being useful, of missing something."

In the first place, as Lee points out, "None of us really had a father around." Don never knew his father, while Jerry rarely saw his father after his early childhood years. Lee might just as well not have known his father, who "sometimes came home just long enough to drop off a suitcase of dirty clothes and pick up a suitcase of clean ones." Lee's experience shows that one does not have to come from a broken family like Don's or Jerry's to feel as if one does:

> What I remember most from childhood is a constant, overwhelming feeling of loneliness. Having plenty of clothes, plenty of toys, but wanting, needing something else that I wasn't getting. It was the other kids' fathers who always took us places, and I saw those fathers at home, playing with their kids. I would daydream about some other family adopting me and taking care of me, a family with a typical Jack Armstrong father who was there to play with me.

Lee's account is strikingly (and surprisingly) similar to Don's in another way as well. Both men feel they did not have a chance to develop skills that would bring them a sense of worth and competence as well as approval and recognition in the family and elsewhere. Social psychologist Isidor Chein has written that "from almost his earliest days, the addict has been systematically educated and trained into incompetence."[1] or as Don tells it:

> There wasn't much room for any responsibility on my part. My mother worked, and my grandmother took care of things in the house. There were no demands on me to do any chores. If I tried to touch a dish — especially if I broke it — my grandmother would say, "Don't let him do it. He can't do anything." My grandmother needed to feel needed in the home. If I did anything, it was like taking something away from her. In her struggle to maintain her own role, my role got lost.

For Lee, over in suburbia, it was the same story:

> Everything either was somebody else's job or was thought to be somehow beyond my capacities. My parents' attitude was, "Don't let him do anything, because if you do he'll break it." They wouldn't let me turn on the garden hose for fear I'd have it pointed in the wrong direction. That left me with a tremendous fear of trying new things. I'd always fear I was going to fail. I was told to get good grades in school, and I did get them, but I lived in mortal fear of failure.

Ironically, he did not fail — outwardly. As we shall see, Lee, Don, and Jerry alike turned out to be highly competent, not only in their professional work but also in their earlier careers of deviance. And Lee all along was highly successful in school and in business as well. What they each lacked was a *sense* of competence, a sense of being able to do things that they could value and that others would appreciate. And when that sense of competence is not present, is not affirmed and reinforced, then one of the three basic living skills that Lee speaks of is missing. A person then may well ask, "Who am I? What am I?"

Don and Jerry grew up with too few rules, Lee with too many. Either way, one doesn't build up an easy confidence in one's capacity to negotiate reality. Instead, there is a restless scramble to outguess a menacing fate, to keep from falling off the deep end, to stay on top of dire but unnameable consequences. In that scramble, as Don tells us, a person's role gets lost — the role of a responsible adult.

Both Don and Lee describe themselves in childhood as "overprotected." Jerry was underprotected, except insofar as he could attach himself to the neighborhood community and its juvenile gangs. In Don's and Jerry's relationships with their mothers (which was especially crucial since both men grew up without a father in the house) there are interesting correspondences as well as contrasts which say something about the origins of addiction. Both women were party-goers who loved a good time and did not find it easy to adjust to having a child. There the resemblences ended. Jerry's mother went on partying until she died. As Jerry tells it, "She played cards for money on her deathbed." Don, on the other hand, had this highly charged memory of his mother:

> My mother told me that one day when I was about five years old she came home from some outing with her crowd and saw me on my tricycle. She took a look at me and said, "That's it. No more of this. I have a son, and I want him to have a good life." On that day, she told me, she let go of everything else and dedicated her life to me.

Her dedication was a heavy burden for her son to carry, perhaps heavier than Jerry's mother's indifference. Don recalls:

> She's a strong person. She worked all those years to support me and my grandmother. And she

> stayed by me through drugs, jail, everything. She gave me a lot of love, put everything into me, and that was both good and not good, because even now it's been really hard to break out to that dependency and learn to be responsible myself.

In her devotion there was a note of self-denial and self-sacrifice, perhaps even matryrdom, that Don picked up and exploited.

> I was spoiled with material things — nice clothing, a bike. I got to go to the movies four or five times a week. After a while I took advantage of this, played it for what it was worth. My mother made the sacrifices; I got the benefits.

Whether Don's mother was trying to make up for partially neglecting him during his first five years, or for not being able to give him a father, one can only speculate. What does seem clear is that she felt a conflict between pleasure and responsibility which she resolved by coming down hard on the side of the latter. Don sensed this conflict; indeed, it has become his conflict as well. As a child he responded by extorting more and more of the "material things" that he felt were being offered as bribes. He developed, in other words, the manipulative, *taking* orientation of the addict-to-be. It was almost as if his mother's guilt gave him an exploitive role to play.

Don's words take us back to Lee's recollection of childhood: "Having plenty of clothes, plenty of toys, but wanting, needing something else that I wasn't getting." In Lee's case a harsh paternal discipline got in the way of his exploring who he was, what he was feeling, what common ground he might have with others. While Don ran from violence in the streets, Lee ran from violence at home. While don was being appeased by his mother's gifts, Lee "would steal things — from my mother, from department stores — and give them away. I did it to buy friends. Buying friends — it's something I did in bars up to the very end of my drinking."

Don and Lee, and Jerry as well, learned to view personal relationships as a tense interplay of fighting and wheedling. As

Isidor Chein and his collaborators have shown in *The Road to H*,[2] a sociological and psychological study of young heroin users in New York, dishonesty,[3] suspicion, and manipulativeness in personal relationships are of the essence of the addictive outlook on life. Whatever else addiction may be, it is an attempt to substitute for the emotional support and the sense of connectedness that people generally get from close personal relationships. When even one's closest relationships are characterized by alienation and materialistic exploitation, there is a gap that one may turn to drugs to fill.

In a revealing aside to his life history, Don has remarked,

> I didn't have an easy feeling among people in the neighborhood because there was a kind of suspicion in our family. I was taught, "Don't let family secrets out of the house." That's what makes it feel a little daring to be relating these things now.

Not surprisingly, Don is still guarded in talking about his life and his feelings. In his account of himself, even more than in Lee's and Jerry's, there are gaps that must be filled in. But the tight-lipped attitude Don cites, a common one in post-World-War-II America, has a more general significance for understanding addiction. As *Love and Addiction* stresses, the preoccupation with hoarding sensitive information makes it hard to form genuine relationships with neighbors, classmates, friends. When those individuals are treated as strangers — in some sense even enemies — potentially valuable relationships may be compromised out of existence. In people who become addicted the same guardedness often makes itself felt in more immediate relationships as well. A persistent theme of Lee's, Don's and Jerry's accounts of their lives before and during addiction is their inability to trust and be honest with their intimates, including their wives.

If there was something unreal about their relationships with people, the same was true of other important aspects of their lives. Don quit school because nothing that went on there interested him. Lee inwardly felt the same way. Don "had no one to give me direction, to help me work out the feelings, the skills — whatever was inside me." Lee, on the other hand, "was given plenty of direction by others, but I didn't feel it. It came from outside me. School and the rest was a script that was written 'for' me." Achievement in school was part of the script; another consisted of "packaged ideas" of "responsibility, the cozy love nest, and ready-made-sex" that were to lead Lee into an early marriage. Lee, every bit as much as Don, felt his life to be taking place somewhere outside himself. He didn't feel it, didn't believe it, didn't trust it. Each time he was successful in school and later in business, he "kept saying to myself that it had to be luck. Because it couldn't be me." Living outside his own experience, he dreaded exposure as a "phony" and a "con man."

Lee thinks of his own early years as a textbook example of the driven existence that Albert Ellis refers to when he speaks of "musts" and "oughts," and that Karen Horney has called "The Tyranny of the Should."[3]:

> My family and my teachers taught me not to feel what I did feel, but what I *should* feel; not to see and hear what was there, but what *should* be there; not to ask for what I wanted, but to wait to be asked; not to take risks, but to protect the status quo. They taught me that I had to take in things from outside — drugs, alcohol, people, sex, work — to feel the way I wanted to inside.

Here Lee draws the connection between the addict's pervasive detachment from experience and his longing for an external "answer." As an adolescent Lee had not yet found his "answer," but he felt all too strongly the detachment, the alienation from himself.

> In high school, going by the "shoulds," I became all the things my self-consciousness and discomfort would lead me to avoid: champion debater, drama club star, extrovert. It was terrible,

> it felt so phony, but I had to do it because I couldn't stand not being part of a group. In a debate I'd always think I was going to lose — I *had* to lose — but I'd win. So I'd think, "Next time they'll catch me, catch on that I'm a phony." All through high school I fought to be one of the crowd, and all along I felt like crying out, "Take me and love me and let me be, and I'll do anything, anything."
>
> College was the same thing. After being at Boston University a month I swore I was going to flunk out. For four years I was on the Dean's List, and always it was the next semester that they were going to catch up with me and flunk me out. When I got my diploma I sincerely believed that they were going to come along and take the damn thing away because I had conned them. Conned my way through high school, through college — a con man since I was a kid.

***

Many of us grow up with "packaged ideas" about love and marriage. Many of us were admonished not to "let family secrets out of the house." Certainly we do not all become addicts. But parents who train us not to desert the warmth and security of our homes for the chaos of mistrust that lurks outside are training us to look for other tiny warm spots in which to hide. A social milieu that gives us the mere externals of experience to latch on to — that teaches us to perceive our experience as being external to ourselves — leaves us with a lack of interest, a lack of enjoyment, a lack of assurance about what we are doing. All of us then become susceptible to addictions to a greater or lesser degree. Those individuals who feel most strongly the pressures of self-doubt and insufficiency are most vulnerable to the easy attractions of an addiction.

It was this vulnerability that Lee, Don, and Jerry felt in their teens. Lee was busy striving to match his father's record of achievement — and vomiting from nervousness when he went out on dates. Don was getting sick, too — from the drinking he did with his high school friends. One night after a sorority party he blacked out on a beach during a storm and "woke up the next day all banged up, knocked off my feet for a week." He was then thirteen years old. Drinking proved so unpleasant that he stopped; so did school, which he left at sixteen.

> I couldn't concentrate. I was very restless. And there was no interest, no stimulation. There was nothing there for me, nothing I wanted to be. So I went to work putting in acoustic tile ceilings. Soon I was making good money, enough to buy a car, clothes, go to dances.

Jerry, who never really went to school in the first place, was letting go of his tenuous ties with straight society and getting himself ensconced in the dark corners of his neighborhood. Although they didn't know it at the time, it was as if all three young men were waiting to find the "high" that would lift them out of their disadvantages and despair.

2
finding the high

In the 1940's the American dream machine was running at full speed. Hollywood was enjoying one of its most expansive decades, radio brought college and professional sports into the nation's living rooms, and the big bands gave young Americans yet another set of heroes. At a time when nearly everyone was escaping into these fantasies, it is not surprising that Lee, Don, and Jerry did, too. Don went to the movies several times a week, Jerry as much as three times a day. Lee sums up what the movies meant to them as well as to himself:

> I was so unhappy with who I was and where I was that I identified with every movie that had a hero — war hero, western hero, existential hero, anything.

"Andy Hardy's father became my father," says Lee, just as John Garfield, George Raft, Robert Taylor, and Edward G. Robinson were models of manhood for Jerry. Jerry made the world of sports his own, learning the name of every player on the Giants and the Yankees, while Lee, who "didn't know which teams were in which leagues," knew the name of every player in every major jazz band in the country. Don, too, was drawn into music, but for him, growing up in the fifties, it was blues and early rock and roll.

> The older crowd I was involved with went everywhere — New York, Massachusetts. At the Roseland Ballroom or the arena up in Holyoke, you could see Fats Domino or B.B. King play all night with a black band. The people there were mostly black, but my friends were from the black areas and knew their way around these dance halls.

There is nothing unusual about any of these activities. But as Lee's comment about the movies illustrates, that which is a momentary escape for most people has a more intense appeal for a person who is looking for a constant or total escape. John Luce speaks for Lee, Don, and Jerry in his case study of "Ed," a heroin addict in San Francisco. When Ed was a child his mother took him to the Saturday matinees at the Haight Theater. "Ed loved sitting in the ancient movie palace," writes Luce. "He felt secured by the thought that life could be stable, relaxed by the celluloid sensations that enveloped him."[1] There is something about the cool, dark, comfortable theater, the soothing atmosphere, the contained environment of the movies that approaches the sensation a habitual user seeks from alcohol or heroin. In the movies Lee, Don, and Jerry found fantasies of a life where problems were more simply resolved than in the tangled reality from which they fled.

If one's problems and conflicts are felt to be external to oneself, so is their solution. As a child, Lee felt that he "had to escape from that loneliness, go somewhere else, even if it was just into fantasy." Jerry uses similar language to describe the addict's "nebulous, superficial conception of happiness":

> To me, happiness was a place where I could go where there would never be any more troubles. It was an unnamed something that other people had and I didn't, a place where other people were

> and I wasn't. I thought of it as a geographical location that you could apply for a passport to. And if happiness was something outside myself, a different place, then the drug, the euphoria, the high was a way of getting there, at least for a time.

***

Adolescence is the time when drug and alcohol use becomes available as an option, a way of getting away from pain. It is also a time when the conflicts that precipitate addictive drug use come to a head. Either one accepts the challenges of emerging adulthood, or one takes a detour. Sociologist Charles Winick, noting that heroin is usually a young person's habit, later to be outgrown, explains:

> The use of narcotics may make it possible for the user to evade, mask, or postpone the expression of these needs and these decisions [i.e., sex, aggression, vocation, financial independence and support of others] . . . On a less conscious level, he may be anticipating becoming dependent on jails and other community resources . . . Becoming a narcotics addict in early adulthood thus enables the addict to avoid many decisions . . .[2]

Winick's speculation finds strong corroboration in Don's recollections of his early incapacity to assume a masculine role. One reason Don gives for quitting school at sixteen was that "I was afraid of the responsibility, afraid of demands being put on me" by his girlfriend.

> She was the first girl I was serious with. Even at fourteen I could sense that she was looking toward getting married because she wanted so badly to get out of her house. And that made me uptight. It focused a lot of my fears at the time.

Freeing himself from this involvement, he "started hanging out with an older crowd and fooling around with older women. I guess I wanted someone else to take the responsibility of leadership and show me how to do things."

One of the things they showed Don how to do was to shoot heroin, which became available in the black music circles that he frequented. Don took his first shot in 1957, at the age of seventeen, after a dawn dance in Holyoke, Massachusetts.

> We all came back to an apartment where people were shooting up. This woman said, "Come on, don't you know what this is about?" I didn't want to seem like a lame head, a square, so I acted like I knew what it was all about. I was scared to death, but I had to make this scene, and I did — I shoved the needle in my arm. I didn't know what I was doing, and I didn't enjoy it. I just acted out what somebody else was doing and what somebody else was telling me to do. I got no kicks out of it, just tension, because I was on the spot, and I couldn't push aside the demands being put on me.

Lee participated in "phony" extracurricular activities because "I couldn't stand not being part of a group." It was with the same lack of personal involvement, the same exaggerated consciousness of social pressure, that Don began taking drugs. It wasn't fun; it was a stressful imposition.

Don's second try occurred under more relaxed conditions, in the company of a friend:

> There was no pressure; it was just the two of us there, and I did it voluntarily, out of my own curiosity. This time I felt it. Everything went away, and a feeling of well-being, of confidence came over me.
>
> Those first couple of bags of heroin gave me a sense of security. The drug was a haven; it gave me peace of mind. It gave me instant relief from all

> the bad feelings, the torments. I felt on top of things, and the fears went away: the fears about women, about work, about my family, about where I belonged and what I was going to do. Just then the drug was the answer to all my problems.

***

Lee was looking for all these things, too. He, too, was looking for an answer to all his problems, but for him the answer could not be heroin, which was "completely foreign" to him. Lee, who is ten years older than Don, grew up in the 1940s. More important, he grew up in a middle-class world. "Marijuana was the worst thing you could even think of when I was a kid," he recalls. "Gene Krupa was picked up for marijuana, and it was like a murder rap. The only thing we knew about narcotics was Chinese opium dens."

People get addicted to drugs that are available among the people they associate with and that are identified by those people as having pain-relieving powers. As a working-class Irish-American Don might well have developed an addiction to alcohol. Yet he did not do so, even though he began drinking at an early age, because he associated less with other Irish-Americans than with youths on the fringes of society who took up the heroin that circulated around black musicians. For Lee the socially acceptable addictive drug was alcohol, the "universal solvent," to which people of all ethnic groups and social classes (albeit in varying proportions) become addicted. For others, including those for whom addictive alcohol use is as unimaginable as shooting heroin was for Lee, the object of addiction may be cigarettes or food.

Lee's road to alcoholism began with medically prescribed barbiturates. In his teens he was given phenobarbitol by his family doctor, "with all the refills I needed," to control his nausea and vomiting when he went out on dates. (To have such an agreeable family doctor is a privilege of the affluent.) At Boston University he was put on Seconal for insomnia during exam periods. He was still taking a handful of phenobarbitols before every date.

Whereas Don and Jerry were "given their wings" (i.e., introduced to heroin) by their peers, Lee was given first barbiturates and then alcohol in the charged atmosphere of his relationship with his father. In 1950, after his sophomore year in college, he had a minor eye operation in New York. The doctor gave him a prescription for a pain-killing drug (probably codeine).

> After I came out of the office I went to a bar with my father and two buddies of mine who had come down with me. I remember it as if I were sitting there now. My father said, "I'd just as soon you didn't take drugs. Why don't you have a drink? That will take the pain away." He ordered me a drink, Canadian Club and orange juice, and I drank it. I didn't say anything, but it was wild. It was every sensation I'd ever looked for, in an instant — instant relief and relaxation.
>
> All the pain and awkwardness vanished with that first drink. The fear, the weakness, the sexual anxiety, the inability to face people — they all disappeared. Imagine what it feels like to live with the anguished memories, the worries and forebodings that I lived with day in and day out. Then imagine what it feels like to have them all dissolve away in a glass of magic liquid. When I looked back on that first drink, I felt like Martin Luther King when he said, "I have been to the mountain." That was the remembered "high" that I chased for twenty years and that others chase as long as they live. That was the "freedom" that it took me twenty years to free myself from.
>
> If that was how the first drink made me feel, what was I going to do when I was offered another? Naturally, I took it. My father took off, and I went out drinking with those two guys. I must have had fifteen or twenty drinks that night.

> It was like gangbusters. I was walking into restaurants where I would normally slink in, and the later the evening got the bigger my chest grew.

"Since alcohol and phenobarbitol are cross-tolerant and cross-dependent," Lee explains, "I was conditioned to be an alcoholic when I took my first drink." He is referring to the fact that alcohol and barbiturates are closely related chemically, so that building up a tolerance to one means building up a tolerance to the other as well (i.e., requiring stronger and stronger doses to achieve the same effect). Similarly, the symptoms of alcohol withdrawal can be relieved by taking a barbiturate, and vice versa. Thus, since Lee had been taking phenobarbitol, it was as if he had already been drinking regularly when he had his first drink.

Cross-tolerance explains how Lee was able to handle fifteen or twenty drinks that evening. It does not explain why he took so many drinks. It may be that the medically prescribed doses of phenobarbitol that he received did not provide a strong enough euphoria to induce him to take more. Or it may be that barbiturates, while soothing, do not give the user the sensation of power ("the bigger my chest grew") that an alcoholic typically craves.[3] The chemistry may have been the same as phenobarbitol, but the *experience* was different from any that Lee had had before. It was that experience that led to his becoming addicted to alcohol.

Lee's father had told him that having a drink "will take the pain away," referring to the pain from minor surgery. But Lee found that the drink took away a much larger pain. He gets to the heart of the matter when he says, "The feeling I got from the booze was the important thing. It took care of all the inadequacies I felt — in intelligence, in sex, everything."

Don uses very similar words to describe what heroin did for him: "I felt grand with women; the bag took all my inadequacies away." Again, it was the feeling that made the difference. Lee's and Don's stories of their first drug experiences are remarkably parallel. Both men use the expression "instant relief." Both say that drugs removed the fears and inadequacies they had felt all their lives.

For both Lee and Don, what mattered about the initial drug experience was that it transported them from one state of being to another. Their words recall those of Lawrence Kolb, a pioneering drug researcher who in the 1920s wrote one of the most perceptive things that has ever been said about addiction. According to Kolb, the people who become addicted are those who "receive from narcotics a pleasurable sense of relief from the realities of life that normal persons do not receive because life is no special burden to them."[4]

***

Jerry's account of his introduction to heroin does not fit Kolb's model. It differs from Lee's or Don's in its matter-of-factness:

> In 1949, when I was fourteen, a new phenomenon hit the neighborhood: dope. There had always been a little pot, but now there was heroin in what were called 5/9 caps. Four people could get off on one of them, which cost a dollar. My first experience came when a bunch of us were sitting around and someone brought in one of those caps. I joined in without any internal debate. It wasn't an issue; it was just the natural thing to do. It made me quite sick, though, and I began to throw up. That was when I made my first bargain with God: "If you let me live, I'll never do this again." Of course, He let me live, and of course, I did it again.

Jerry does not say that existence was painful for him and that the pain led to his drug use. He does not say much about whatever pain he may have felt. So he was short and skinny with big ears; so are many adolescent boys. So he had been essentially abandoned by both his parents; some of the friends who shared those first "caps" with him had intact nuclear families. As Jerry tells it, he began taking heroin "for fun" and without any great fanfare. His description of the narcotic "high" is correspondingly moderate and low-key:

> Physically and mentally I felt relaxed, laid back. I felt a certain release that at the same time I knew was only temporary. It was a feeling that the pressure was off me, that all was right with the world. My quest was to reach that state of well-being by getting high, and the feeling included the awareness that at some point the quest would have to start again.

The drug that could produce this reaction is recognizably the same drug that Don took, yet Jerry's reaction was much less intense. That such differences are possible is an important fact to note in understanding addiction.

Lee has questioned Jerry closely about what his feeling of well-being was and why it meant so much to him. If Jerry wanted this good feeling enough to shoot up in order to get it, Lee suggests, he must have felt bad in the first place. Jerry's reply is that he successfully "masked" or "blocked" whatever bad feelings he had as an adolescent. If he had reason to be dissatisfied with his life, he didn't want to think about it.

In rejecting any intrapsychic explanation of his drug use, Jerry does offer another explanation. "At the time," he says, "the only motivation I was aware of was a desire to belong. Here was a group that was willing to accept me, and this was the criterion for being accepted." In other words, heroin use was simply a natural outgrowth of his involvement with a delinquent group. It was a badge of membership in a deviant subculture, not a way of relieving the pain of existence. At the time, of course, he did not think of it as "deviant." It was just "the thing to do."

***

Thus far we have seen how the novice drug user backs into a negativistic solution — whether in flight from responsibilities he can't handle, like Don; to ease the pain of assuming responsibilities he finds agonizing, like Lee; or, like Jerry, as a substitute for responsibilities he hardly knows exist. As Don puts it,

> When I was young, I found something that I called magic, a secret that took away the pain of existence. From my second or third bag I knew that the feeling was so good that I was going to get it whatever the price. I chased that bag for ten years.

"Finding the secret of the high," agrees Lee. "That's what it's all about."

> Whatever happened to my childhood resolve never to touch a drink? I forgot it, I guess. I forgot for the next twenty years. To this very minute I can remember the high I got from my first drink. Most people I know can remember their first high. You're always chasing that remembered high, like an orgasm. It's something you know that nobody else does.

Jerry, too, had found the secret of the high, which he describes with characteristic modesty. "Happiness was a Sunday morning wake-up," he recalls. "It was knowing that you had scored enough on Saturday that you didn't have to go out and hustle on Sunday."

3
getting high

The largest and most common misconception people have about addiction is the idea that it is directly caused by some property of a drug. Addiction is not so simple as that. It is not a chemical reaction, but an experience. It is, as Jerry says, a relationship that a person has with a drug or other addictive object. And there are two sides to a relationship. To quote the apt title of a book by Eugene Kaplan and Herbert Wieder, "Drugs don't take people. People take drugs."[1] Whether something is addictive depends on how a person uses it. Nothing — even heroin or alcohol — is inherently addictive, although some things (like heroin and alcohol) lend themselves particularly well to experiences which can become addictive. Nothing — even a good old all-American love affair — is inherently *not* addictive. Some people are susceptible to being addicted to any number of things; some are hardly susceptible to any.

Who is susceptible? In Lawrence Kolb's words, it is the person who receives from a particular drug or experience "a pleasurable sense of relief from the realities of life." We recall Lee's comment: "All the pain and awkwardness vanished with that first drink, so when I was offered another drink, I took it." In that "so" lies the dynamic of addiction. If a particular sensation makes such a marked difference in the way a person feels about himself and his situation, the person will naturally want to repeat that sensation in order to go on having the good feelings rather than the bad. And so the story of addiction begins with the repeated quest for the good feelings, the ones that come from "getting high."

***

At first there are only good feelings. Certainly it was that way for Don. All he had to do was look around him at his companions to see that heroin didn't really cause people's bodies to deteriorate or their teeth to fall out. Nor did it interfere with his life. Even when he was partying all weekend every weekend in Hartford or New York — with four or five bags of dope to keep the party going — he was able to work during the week. Since heroin in the fifties was still relatively inexpensive, Don was able to support his weekend habit on the money he earned.

"Living in the present, going strictly by my feelings," Don found that heroin, far from interfering with his life, seemed to enhance it.

> I was making the jazz scene from the Village to Copley Square in Boston. And Newport — I remember seeing George Shearing and Ray Charles there in '58. I didn't need to get off during the day, but it was nice to get off in the evening and go sit and enjoy the music, enjoy the breeze coming in off the ocean. It made me feel special, back there in the fifties. I didn't need to carry a bottle in there; I was in my own little world with the music.

Meanwhile, though, his habit was growing from a weekend to an everyday affair. He began missing days of work to hustle dope. But even when he quit work altogether and supported himself instead by passing bad checks, he still could characterize his life as "fun and excitement."

> I was healthy; drugs hadn't affected me much, and there were no tell-tale marks on my body. My days were full, and there was no more boredom. I was free to nod and dream day in and day out, to float above all the bullshit.

He did not understand the significance of his assumption that life before drugs, and life without drugs, was "boredom." Since he always had dope he didn't realize that he needed it. For this same reason many people never realize that they are addicted to cigarettes or coffee or to a dependent love relationship — until it ends.

When the arrests began — first for bad checks, then for stealing doctors' bags to get morphine or Demerol — Don faced a potentially serious situation. "Back in the fifties and early sixties you could get big time for drug busts," he recalls. "My bonds were five, ten thousand dollars — today they'd be two hundred." However, by refusing to implicate anyone besides himself he kept the support of his fellow users and his connections, and he made bond each time with their help or with that of his mother, whose support was (and has remained) unconditional. Once he was free from custody, he forgot about the court hearing he faced. "Just get high again, get some dope in me, and everything will take care of itself."

> It was a game, a fantasy thing — cops and robbers. I thought I could call "Cut!" and walk right out of it any time I wanted. Like when I was pinched in Manchester for snatching doctors' bags. I was sent to Norwich State Hospital for thirty days' observation, and then I went before probate court. The normal procedure was for them to keep you a lot longer than thirty days — more like six months. But I knew I had it made. My hair was cut, and my eyes were focused right

> again; I was the young innocent kid. I went before that Board and looked them right in the eye — a judge and two doctors. I told them, "These thirty days have been a real experience for me. Now I know what I was getting myself into. I want to get back home now and resume my education. My mother's working, my grandmother's there with her, and I want to help them out." And I sold them on it. I had them sewed up. They let me walk right out of there.

He still didn't know that he was hooked. But he was beginning to get intimations, as when he and his friends made their runs to New York.

> Our main connection there was a black couple living in a filthy apartment — roaches all over, dishes piled up, the kids greasy and dirty. The man and the woman were both using drugs, and the woman, a light-skinned black who I thought was beautiful, was a prostitute turning tricks there in the apartment. For me it was a frightening glimpse of a new world, a preview.

"Chasing dope full-time," he saw the drug scene come into his home.

> Before that I always did drugs somewhere else; I'd always have a sanctuary to come home to. When I lost that, when drugs started to pervade my life,. a lot of the enjoyment and excitement went out of it. It was a full-time job now, and I had to be good at it. I'd wake up at three in the afternoon, go out, stay out all night, score, and come back for a few hours' sleep before going out again the next afternoon. That became my role, my identity.

"More and more it became work," he relates. The fun had lasted perhaps six months or a year.

***

Lee, too, began with a weekend habit. He thought there was a rule that drinking was for weekends and weekends were for drinking, while weekdays were for staying in a "shell" and studying. That was how he spent his last two years of college. Even then, though, he could never stop drinking once he had started. "Right from the beginning I knew I didn't drink the way other people did. They'd sit there sipping, and I'd be three drinks ahead of them." The frenzy of weekend socializing was a pretext. "Drinking was the most important activity I had in my spare time."

After Lee graduated from Boston University and went to the Harvard Business School his drinking expanded, as had Don's drug use, from his spare time to work time. He was blacking out more frequently. He smashed up a car — the first in a long line of wrecks he was to leave behind over the years. His drinking affected his grades. Following the Business School's recommendation, he went to a psychologist (neglecting, of course, to say anything about his drinking).

> My going to a psychologist resolved everything neatly for the school. It meant that the school was discharging its responsibility for my welfare, and that I was cooperating nicely. So all would be forgiven. Now I really *was* a con man.

This was just after a poignant moment for Lee. Like many another high school boy, Lee had idolized a popular girl with whom he didn't have the nerve to speak — indeed, had built her up into an unapproachable love goddess. For him, however, the story took an unusual turn when he met her again while home from college on a holiday. For the first time they really talked, and he invited her to his Senior Prom. "We spent a chaste weekend together in Boston, staying in adjoining rooms and hanging out the windows to talk. Back home we drank together all summer."

The couple faced two obstacles. The woman was already committed to a boyfriend who was away, and she and Lee were of different faiths, which meant that their relationship was opposed by her parents as well as his. They might have overcome these obstacles if they had had a kind of courage that not many young couples possessed in 1952. As Lee recalls, "I kept hoping that it would work out, but I didn't do anything to make it happen. I couldn't face the confrontation with my parents. It was easier just to let it pass." This was how it was for the woman, too. Although she and Lee both felt the strength of the love that brought them together, they both chose to yield to the forces that kept them apart. With sorrow they turned away from each other. It was many years before they could face seeing each other again.

Having backed away from this confrontation, having yielded to his father again by going to the Harvard Business School (instead of the Army, where he thought he could get away from his sorrow), Lee was spoiling for a fight. During his first year at Harvard, while still "on the rebound," he met his first wife, Doris. She, too, could drink with him, and he was looking for constant companionship. Although he knew he wasn't ready for marriage, Lee locked himself into a defiant stance toward his father by immediately announcing his intentions. Thus, after a six-week courtship, he jumped into a marriage that began as it was to end — in the office of a marriage counselor.

When Lee received his M.B.A. he and Doris moved back to Manchester. In a conscious effort to break out of his father's high-pressure mold he took a $3100-a-year teaching job in the labor relations department at the University of Connecticut. He and Doris couldn't live for very long on that salary, however. In 1955, after a year of teaching, Lee went into the insurance business with a partner and became an overnight success. Yet still he could not believe in the reality of his accomplishments.

> My partner and I opened beautiful offices and did everything first-class. I was a natural salesman, a great one, but I always felt as if the customer was going to cancel the policy as soon as I was out the

> door. It was like back in school — that refusal to accept success, that sense of impending failure. Still, it seemed I couldn't help but be successful.

By now his business and personal life were thoroughly subordinated to his drinking. Seeing the importance of entertainment in the insurance business, he "lived in bars" with customers. He also was active in civic and political affairs.

> I was a bigshot in sixteen different organizations, getting all kinds of awards — all as a cover for my drinking. Between the business and community work I'd take on as much pressure as I could possibly bear, in order to justify the amount of drinking and entertaining I was doing. If I got smashed at the annual polio fund dinner after turning out a record-breaking fund-raising job, people would say, "Well, after all, he's worked so hard on this."

Socially, he gravitated towards heavy drinkers "so I'd have an excuse to bring the bottle out. Their drinking became the rationale for mine."

> I was up for work at seven every morning and out getting drunk every night until one or two o'clock. I admitted that drinking was a problem, but it still felt too good to do anything about it. So I'd hide it.. I'd be drunk with different people at different times so that nobody would know I was always getting drunk. If I got drunk at a party one Saturday night, I'd go to a party with a different crowd the next week. I was still the same phony I was in school. I was convinced that people accepted me only because they hadn't caught up with me yet, and I wasn't about to let them catch up.
>
> I protected my reputation with constant entertainment. Sometimes I had people in my home for

> dinner Friday, Saturday, and Sunday evenings. My wife was going crazy; she didn't want all that. But it surrounded me with people who were also drinking, and it kept me from being alone. For me it was terrifying to be alone, as a kid and as an adult. Eating dinner, for example, was something I just couldn't do alone. So if Doris wasn't home or if I was on a business trip, I'd go for days without dinner.

With two young children to take care of, Doris couldn't handle this level of "stimulation." She and Lee decided on a six-week separation just when he was about to leave for Florida to look over the prospects for opening a branch office there.

> The night before I left I got a brand new convertible and smashed it up coming back from a party. Totalled it with 167 miles on it. I'll never forget that convertible — a red Chrysler, fully equipped, with real black leather upholstery. Yet I forgot it easily enough that night — just left it there and got a ride home. The next day I picked up another new car and was on my way. Discarded one four-thousand-dollar car (the equivalent of twelve thousand today) and picked up another as if I were changing a tie. Already I was into the insanity that was to be so evident ten years later at the end of my drinking. I just watched it all happen, as if it didn't mean a thing.
>
> All the way down to Florida I gave serious thought to changing my ways. This was a time, I told myself, when I could really put myself together.

During his twenty years of drinking Lee tried many techniques for controlling his drinking: hobbies, vitamin formulas, psychiatrists, hospitalizations, "going dry" for a month or two, limiting the number of drinks he would take, switching from hard liquor to beer or wine, changing his business or family situation — everything but the simplest trick of all, that of just stopping. In 1959, the midpoint of those twenty years, we see him trying one of the most common of these evasions — geographical change. An already desperate attempt to moderate what is in its very nature immoderate, it was to fail for one simple reason: When you move, you take yourself along. If you don't change yourself, it doesn't matter where you go. Whatever Lee was in Connecticut, that was what he would be in Florida.

***

For Jerry the good feelings came from being one of the "hopheads," as heroin users were called in his community, rather than one of the "faggots," or straight kids. For the "hopheads" back in the late forties there was little strain connected with obtaining and using the drug.

> We didn't have to go searching for heroin; it came our way. And it wasn't much of a problem to hustle up a quarter or fifty cents for the three or four of us. Still, we used to sit around wide-eyed when the older "hopheads" reminisced about being able to buy heroin over the counter by brand name before 1914.

As for the "faggots," the word had nothing to do with homosexuality. As Jerry puts it, "'Faggot' was my catch-all term for anyone I didn't like or wasn't comfortable with, anyone who disagreed with me" — including some people in his own family.

Both the "hopheads" and the "faggots" were Jewish; *everybody* in that neighborhood was Jewish. Jerry grew up in the kind of milieu described in Irving Howe's *World of Our Fathers*, a self-contained Jewish community of recent immigrants and their offspring. This community contained a whole spectrum of character types, including prostitutes, gangsters, and other deviants. It was sufficiently diverse to absorb someone like Jerry's mother, who led a life (gambling, having children out of wedlock) that certainly did not fit the Molly Goldberg image. Jerry's account of his background reminded Lee of Portnoy's visit to Israel in Philip Roth's *Portnoy's Complaint*. When Portnoy got to Israel he was surprised to find that Jews could be porters as well as farmers and teachers. Similarly, there are many Jewish alcoholics and drug addicts (just as there are many middle-class, non-criminal black heroin users) who are not visible to the outside world.

As the "hopheads" branched out from taking drugs to taking other people's cars, Jerry's activities came to the attention of the police. After his second arrest for car theft at the age of sixteen he was given an indefinite minority sentence to Elmira Reformatory in upstate New York. He faced the prospect of staying in Elmira until he was twenty-one unless the court chose to release him sooner.

This first imprisonment was not a crisis for Jerry. His account of this phase of his life portrays an adept, exuberant delinquent "gaming" as imaginatively inside prison walls as he had on the outside.

> Putting me in Elmira was like putting Br'er Rabbit in a briar patch. No problem. I was still very short, and the guys took me in as kind of a pet. At recreation time I'd play handball with the white guys while the black guys played basketball. I felt I belonged there, and it became a home for me — ironically, much more so than the so-called home for Jewish children in Peekskill.
>
> I knew I wasn't going anywhere, so I settled down and adjusted. I found out very quickly how to get what I wanted in that milieu. The barter commodity of the prison was cigarettes, which I accumulated in great quantities by selling food, gambling, and hustling generally. I was also learning new trades such as burglary and passing bad checks. I had a group I could identify with that liked me and appreciated my skills. When had I ever had anything better?

Elmira also was where Jerry finally learned to read and write.

> One of the guards, a local farmer who had taken the job to make some extra money, got out the multiple-choice reading test on which I had guessed well enough to be labelled "dull normal." From the way I manipulated that environment I didn't look "dull normal" to this guard, so he guessed what my problem was. He showed me a *Daily News* headline and said, "Hey, Jerry, what do you think of this?" Well, I wasn't about to admit that I couldn't read. I mean, here I was keeping philosophy and psychology books in my cell to let people know how smart I was. I bluffed him for a while, but eventually he got me to admit it, and to this day I am indebted to him, as well as to a dedicated woman who ran a special program where I learned to read phonetically. One of the first books I read was one of the Hardy Boys mysteries, and it was like a new world to me.

In 1952 the inmates of Elmira were offered a chance to volunteer for the Korean War. Jerry, then seventeen, volunteered. If he stuck it out and got an honorable discharge, his sentence would be set aside. Otherwise he would be sent back to Elmira. Jerry volunteered in part from patriotic motives; he had picked up from the movies the image of the all-American deviant who redeems himself in the war. And although he was comfortable in Elmira, by then he wanted to get out. He couldn't live in a male world forever.

In the Air Force Jerry was trained as a dental technician. Again he manipulated the role of "pet" or "mascot" that he had had in his neighborhood social clubs and in Elmira.

> "Academia," so to speak, was new to me, but I passed with a lot of help from my fellow students, who thought me something of an oddity. As a strategic move I began to come out as a wit, a

> comic, and the instructors were too kind to fail me.

After waiting out the last months of the war far south of the combat zone in Korea, Jerry was transferred to Japan, where he lived luxuriously for the next two years.

> Japan was the Garden of Eden revisited. The dope, houseboys making my bed, PX's and hospitals and officers' and enlisted men's clubs to burglarize. Oh, God, where had this been all my life? I had many sexual adventures with women, some of them more romantic than others. I acquired a bicycle, some clothes, a girlfriend to live with, and a great field for practicing the felonious skills I had learned at Elmira. All along I was using drugs and dealing from native sources. I had a great time, accumulated some money, and had visions of spending the rest of my life in Japan.

He got away with his drug use and drug dealing because these activities were so uncommon that the authorities were not on the lookout for them.

> Something that would be obvious today was not recognized for what it was in 1954. From time to time the military authorities would pick me up and question me about how, if I was making one hundred dollars a month, I could be sending five hundred home to my mother to set aside for me (which she did). But by then I was sophisticated to their questioning. I said I had won the money gambling, and there was nothing they could do.

What they could do was to deny Jerry's request for an extension of his tour of duty in Japan. Jerry hid out with his girlfriend for a week until the Air Police came and put him in handcuffs. They took him to the ship that was leaving for the States from Yokohama and put him in the brig until the ship was out of the harbor. Then they let him upstairs. It was a fitting departure for an accomplished renegade.

When Jerry was honorably discharged from the service a year later at the age of twenty-one, he went back to the Bronx and fell in with his old companions. In the five years since he was sent to Elmira he had gained three inches in height and considerable sexual sophistication. None of his peers had lived with a woman for a year as he had done in Japan.

He came back with greater maturity and self-confidence, and he was going to need every bit of it. The drug scene — the scene into which Don was to be initiated a year later — was out in the open now, and it was a lot tougher. Jerry's neighboorhood was no longer exclusively Jewish, and heroin didn't find its way into the neighborhood as it had before. One had to go to Harlem to get it. In 1956 and 1957 the word "junkies" came into common use through films like *The Man With the Golden Arm*, *Hatful of Rain*, and *Monkey on My Back* — which, as Jerry correctly points out, "were complete myths. I mean, that kind of thing just didn't happen." What did happen was a greater focus on drugs — a hostile focus — by society as a whole. Those who wanted to become involved had to be much more aware and alert. At that point, says Jerry, "junk became the focus of my life."

* * *

Each of these three stories begins with the quest for good feeling and ends on a note of foreboding. At the point where we have left them in this chapter, Don, Lee and Jerry were getting hooked, and they were beginning to realize it. The drug, be it heroin or alcohol, was taking over their lives.

What they didn't realize when they set out after the "high" was that addiction takes a form of a cycle. An addictive involvement with a drug or other experience not only *follows* the pattern of a person's other relationships, but increasingly *sets* the pattern. When a person turns to a drug because something is lacking in his relationships — with people, with work, with pleasure — the effects of the drug (and the effects of using the drug) reinforce and confirm the person's lack of positive involvement and satisfaction in those relationships. Where, then, can the person turn, except to further, more desperate use of the drug? When Lee turned to Don and said, "Addiction was the same thing for both of us," he was stating the essential truth about addiction — that a progressively deepening involvement with any addictive medium marks a progressively worsening relationship with life.

The addiction cycle operates through the "hook" of withdrawal. The power of the withdrawal experience as an impetus to further drug use is well known. What withdrawal really signifies is not nearly so well known. It is worth taking a close look at how withdrawal works, for by understanding withdrawal we can get a new understanding of addiction.

We can begin by looking at situations where withdrawal in the usual sense is not even present — that is, where the addict returns to drug use after a period of being drug-free or, in the case of the alcoholic, "dry." A number of times in his career Don spent several months to a year in prison or (more often) in state hospitals in Connecticut or the federal drug rehabilitation center in Lexington, Kentucky. Drugs were not available to him in these institutions. Each time he got out, he had long since detoxed and therefore was not feeling any physical withdrawal distress. In a comparable situation, U.S. servicemen who had been addicted to heroin in Vietnam and who had detoxed before returning to the States almost never used the drug again once they got home.[2] Yet Don, once outside institutional walls, usually chose to resume drug use within a month or two.

Of this first such relapse he says, "That was when the blow hit me that I couldn't quit dope," using the word "quit" even though he was not at this time actively dependent on the drug.

> A feeling of nothingness came over me. What did I beat that rap for? A janitor was all I'd ever be. Then I decided that I was just not going to go on feeling like that. As long as I couldn't have the life I wanted, I'd adjust myself to shooting dope

> again. If I was going to be nothing, at least I'd feel the way I wanted to feel, not the way I felt naturally.

To the doctors who told him to stop using drugs, he replied:

> It was easy for them to say that; they were warm and comfortable and had some meaning in their lives. They didn't know how I felt without drugs. They only saw me when I was on drugs; I don't think they would have recognized me in my natural state.

He was, in effect, a different person. Lee uses much the same language to convey his inability to stay away from alcohol even when he was not responding to immediate withdrawal distress:

> A couple of times when I went dry, I'd go to a psychiatrist after a few months and tell him quite sincerely that I'd rather be drunk again than go on with the kind of feelings I was living with. What was I ever going to give up booze for — to go back to living with those feelings?

Again, it is generally understood that such motivations as these are important in deciding whether a person begins or resumes drug use. When a person discovers that a particular sensation — the "high" — can change his life, even after periods of abstinence the memory of that sensation will bring him back to the place where he found it, as long as the problems in living that brought him there in the first place are not resolved. It is not so well understood that these same motivations are just as crucial to the process of active, continued drug use. A person takes a second shot, or a second drink (and a third, and a fourth, and so on), to avoid returning to the fear and anxiety that preceded the first.

Not only that, but as time goes on the prospect of returning to that original emotional state becomes more and more painful to contemplate, given the more serious nature of the consequences to be faced the longer reality has been avoided. For Don, the early euphoria of narcotic use meant that "there was no more boredom. I was free to nod and dream day in and day out, to float above all the bullshit." But what happens when the "bullshit" becomes reality again? While the user has been nodding and dreaming, he hasn't been doing anything about the problems in his life. When he comes off the drug, the problems are still there, and he's that much older besides. He's wasted that much more of his life. He may be without money, without a job, without education, without close personal ties; indeed, he may have lost some of these things while he was "afloat" on the drug. And the longer the drug has insulated him from consciousness of these deficiencies, the harder it is, by contrast, to accept them again.

Whenever Don came off drugs (or came out of the protective environment of a prison or hospital, which kept him from using drugs and also from having to manage his own life), he was faced with an untenable situation.

> When I got out, I still had to reassert an identity, find a job, establish relationships, and I couldn't do those things without the pain, the sensitivity, making itself felt. So I went back to the secret potion that would take away that discomfort.

Most of the G.I.'s who used heroin to ease the pain of the untenable situation in which they found themselves in Vietnam did not have such a hard time finding an identity, a job, or relationships back home, and so they didn't need the "secret potion." Other choices were more readily available to them than to Don. The choice between addiction and life is summed up nicely in a story that Don tells:

> There were three of us who started out together. One guy went along with me for a couple of years and then decided that the bag of dope wasn't worth giving up the things in life he wanted, so he

> cut it loose, and he never got messed up the way I did. The other guy is still on the street today.

The lack of those other things in life, the implicit belief that life is "boredom" and "bullshit," the fear of being alone or the fear of being with others — that is the real "hook" of heroin and other addictions.

Don was great at manipulating prison and hospital situations, but "when it came to the longer haul — going to school and getting training for real work — the old nervousness, the old indecision" drove him back to "the path of least resistance," i.e., drug use. Part of the appeal of narcotics or alcohol for a person in flight from responsibility is that it enables him to feel free to be irresponsible. Faced with court hearings, Don's reaction was, "Just get high again, get some dope in me, and everything will take care of itself." Regarding the consequences of his drug use, he says, "I don't think I thought about anything." This is one of the reasons why a person's objective situation often worsens during a prolonged drug "high." Lee tells of many flights of self-destructive irrationality that he indulged in when he made business decisions while drinking. After the euphoria is over, those consequences become clear. Don's arrest record immediately disqualified him from most jobs, so that he was, in effect, "thrown back on drug hustling." The alcoholic may wake up from a binge to find that his wife or his employer has given up on him. Such developments are part of the self-sustaining cycle of addiction.

Lee identifies another key dimension of the addiction cycle when he talks about the shame and guilt engendered by habitual, escapist drug use: "The more you degenerate, the more you hate yourself and the more you have to drink just to live with yourself." Don echoes this sentiment repeatedly. "Once it came home to me that I didn't have drugs beat," he says, "I wasn't the cool, slick dope fiend anymore. I was a defeated dope fiend." When a person takes drugs, as Don did, "so I wouldn't have to face myself," he knows at some level that that is what he's doing. Part of him still knows what's going on. When the effect of the drug wears off, the self he has to face is further reduced in stature, further damaged in his own eyes. This, on top of his worsened external situation, provides yet another reason to want to escape again.

While the addict's self-respect is being eroded through these experiences of futility, he learns to dread even more the power of narcotics or alcohol, a power over *himself* which is demonstrated every time he yields to the impulse to get high again. The effect a drug has on a person is partly a matter of what the person expects from the drug. Such expectations, with different drugs, have varied considerably in different parts of the world and in different historical periods. They also vary greatly among individuals. In the "chemophilic society" that Lee speaks of in *Consider the Alternative,* the message is reinforced on many levels that psychoactive drugs offer an easy way to relax and escape from tension, whether socially or in solitude. Drugs are accorded considerable potency in America, both creative and destructive. Many people keep this force pretty well within bounds because it is balanced by other powerful forces in their lives — interests, values, relationships. But the highly vulnerable individual who lacks these supports to his identity, and whose perception of himself is one of weakness and inadequacy, is likely to be in awe of the drug — and the drug experience — that he is driven to seek out. If we go back to Don's and Lee's accounts of their initial experiences with the substances to which they later became addicted, and the enormous impact they immediately felt from these substances, we find near-religious evocations of a larger-than-life experience. The belief that a drug has the power to addict — that one is powerless to resist it — follows naturally from the belief that a drug can totally transform one's state of being. The two myths go together. A magic potion that can do so much *for* you can work just as powerfully *against* you. It can become a monster that gets inside you and takes over control of your life.

In childhood Lee formed a healthy (or unhealthy) respect for alcohol when he observed what it did to his father's temperament. For years he never tasted a drop. Then, after one drink, he went from one extreme to the other. His outsized fear of the substance turned into an outsized dependency. It was as if his first drink confirmed (in reverse) everything he had learned to believe about the potency of alcohol. His later experience as an alcoholic, of course, directly fulfilled the expectations about alcohol that he had formed in childhood. With regard to heroin, too, we can see the effects of socially induced expectations. Jerry, who was introduced to heroin in a matter-of-fact way by knowledgeable comrades in the late 1940's, when the drug was cheap and easily available, always had an easier time withdrawing than did Don, who picked up the habit in the more tense atmosphere of the late 1950's, when people really believed in the all-powerful narcotic portrayed in *The Man With the Golden Arm.*

Jerry emphatically debunks the "kicking cold turkey" myth. "Withdrawal," he reports, "was like a mild case of the flu." Don, too, describes withdrawal as a matter of being sick for a few days, but he portrays this as a larger, more profoundly traumatic experience. The difference seems to be a generational one. It has been observed that withdrawal symptoms are more strongly expressed and more strongly *felt* when they are indulged.[3] Ironically, they are more likely to be indulged in prison than in tough-minded treatment programs like Daytop Village. In Jerry's early days as a heroin user, the prison environment was more like Daytop than it is now. There was no treatment and considerable opprobrium attached to narcotic withdrawal. To avoid revealing himself as an addict, Jerry withdrew on his own when he started his first prison term. Much to his surprise, he survived the experience quite well.

> When I kicked my first habit I had been using drugs in large amounts — a couple of bags a day — for six months. My stomach turned, my nose dripped, and my head ached. I had cramps in my legs and a dry taste in my mouth. At no time, however, did I think I was going to die. In a couple of days I was feeling myself again, and that's when I started to question the "cold turkey" myth. It became a joke among us: "kicking cold turkey — ha ha ha." Barbiturates, though, were another matter. If any drug scared us, it was barbiturates. Heroin and cocaine did not scare me and my peers, but we stayed away from barbiturates.

Reminded that the federal government in the early 1970s had announced that barbiturates are more dangerous than narcotics in terms of deaths associated with their use (especially deaths from withdrawal), Jerry declared, "We in the Bronx were fifteen years ahead of the federal government!"

Jerry's experience, when placed beside Don's and Lee's, illuminates the nature of withdrawal and its place in the addictive process. Stanton Peele and I have become controversial for having argued in *Love and Addiction* that (as people often paraphase us) "physiological addiction does not exist." One near-hysterical radio talk show host repeatedly asked us in an outraged tone, "Have you ever seen an addict go through withdrawal?" We never said, of course, that addicts don't go through withdrawal. We said that they don't have to. The extreme behavior that is popularly known as heroin withdrawal (and that Jerry lampoons) is a learned response to pain, and not just physical pain.

A more accurate paraphrase would be that addiction is not primarily a matter of physiology. Physiological habituation to a drug is responsible for only a small part of the *behavioral* phenomenon known as addiction, which manifests itself in areas (e.g., gambling, overeating, love) where no chemical bonding can be claimed. Consider the outlandish symptomatology and behavior sometimes shown by jilted lovers or the bereaved — people who temporarily feel as if they have lost the entire basis of their existence. Add to these moderate fever, upset stomach, headache, and cramps, and you have an idea what narcotic withdrawal feels like.

The physical symptoms of withdrawal, in themselves quite mild and hardly noticeable to some people, have an intimidating effect on those who become addicted because they are associated with layers and layers of anxiety and emotional need that the addict desperately wants to keep buried. The men whose life stories are told in this book went back to using drugs or alcohol countless times after (usually enforced) periods of abstinence. It could hardly be claimed that this was a physiological reaction. But even while they were actively addicted, their need to keep using a drug was motivated by the same factors as when they were just starting out or coming back after a layoff: feelings of fear and inadequacy, a lack of close ties with others, an unfavorable situation in life, and a sense of shame that was reinforced by their drug use.

Even those who have never been addicted to drugs or alcohol know what it is like to exaggerate the meaning of a minor illness. When you're laid up with the flu, it's easy to brood about problems that you don't feel strong enough to do anything about. While you're lying in bed, you may well imagine that you will never be able to get up and cope with those problems. Unlike the addict, though, you know from experience that you will regain your strength and that the problems will again become manageable.

If your condition is one that responds to antibiotics, you may be tempted to take a "shot" to make the symptoms go away quickly. But the illness will eventually clear up whether or not you take the shot. Similarly, the addict's withdrawal illness will run its course in a few days even if he does not take his "shot." But for him there is a more serious, chronic illness that will not go away. The addict's normal state of being is as painful psychologically as the withdrawal illness is physically.

Post-operative patients in hospitals often hardly notice that they are going through withdrawal from strong, regularly administered doses of morphine.[4] Like Jerry, Ron LeFlore, the habitual heroin user who later became a major league baseball player, was able to go through withdrawal in prison with relatively little discomfort.[5] Some physicians habitually take morphine or Demerol without showing much tolerance or losing effectiveness in their work.[6] All of these people, despite having some specific reason for relying on drugs, live in a larger world than the one that revolves around the drug "high." For them, "a mild case of the flu" is just that.

For the addict, on the other hand, it is a dire experience. It is a total shock to his system — physical, psychological, social. For someone who is addicted to a drug in the full sense of the word, withdrawal means losing, as Lee puts it, one's only real companion, "this thing that was the answer to everything." Lee found that alcohol withdrawal was never as bad physically as withdrawal from sleeping pills (just as Jerry's heroin-using crowd was wary of barbiturates). In response to Don's questioning, Lee makes light of the "shakes" from alcohol withdrawal as something he routinely got out of the way by hospitalizing himself. Don then asks, "You didn't like giving it up, then." And Lee replies, "When I gave it up I felt like shit."

4
staying even

This is the story of addiction. First you take something so you'll feel good. Then you take it because if you don't you'll "feel like shit" — as not only Lee and Don, but also many ex-smokers and jilted lovers will testify. The pleasure of the "high" fades with time, and the negative after-effect grows. Now you drink or shoot up (or whatever) to keep from getting sick, to avoid re-entry into what seems a clouded, unclean atmosphere. You're no longer ahead of the game; you're just running to stay even. The addiction, which originated in the impulse to avoid pain, has come full circle.

Everyone has to make choices about how to deal with pain. People who have had good lessons in love and trust and successful experiences early in life are more likely not to choose addiction. The prevalence of addictions in our society (including varying degrees of overeating and the routine reliance on caffeine, nicotine, and unhealthy personal relationships) shows that most people are not so fortunate as to approximate this ideal. In any case, whichever choice you make has consequences. If you choose to look at things in the positive, realistic way recommended by Albert Ellis and William Glasser (as explained in Chapter 7), you must live with pain in the short run to have a chance of doing something about it in the long run. If you choose drugs and other mechanisms of avoidance, you can do away with the pain first, but you end up increasing it. For addiction is a three-stage process. In the first stage, it keeps the pain away by making you feel good. In the second, it makes you work hard to keep the pain away. In the third, it makes you feel the pain — but good.

***

Donald Pet, a psychiatrist who (as will be told later) had a great deal to do with the recovery stories recounted in this book, has extensively observed the three stages of addiction in urban heroin addicts[1]. The first stage, he reports, is one of experimentation and "kicks." As Don Flanagan observed among his friends, not everyone who begins using heroin passes into the second stage of more serious use. Some give it up altogether or go on to long-term irregular use. (Non-addictive heroin use is a greatly underpublicized phenomenon in America.) Those who do go on to the second stage become dependent on the drug, lose control over their use of it, and (under present conditions) usually choose a criminal lifestyle.

Don himself was one of those who passed quickly into the second stage.

> I knew that the drug had taken control about a year or two into my addiction, about '58 or '59. Before that it had always been part of something, had always enhanced something, like jazz or going out to dinner with someone. But when it became just part of sitting on a couch with my head between my legs, then I knew something had happened. The drug started to dominate when it became the end in itself, when I lost interest in the things the drug had helped me appreciate. I stop-

> ped getting involved with people. I stopped going to parties and dances. I lost interest in music, clothes, my appearance. People saw that something was different when I didn't change my pants for a month. If someone mentioned the Newport Jazz Festival, I'd say, "Yeah, that's great," but there was no way I was going to get there. And if I did, I'd have to make sure I had enough stuff to last me. That was all that mattered.

Don had made a choice to let the drug "take control" of his life. How far he was prepared to go to maintain that choice and what further desperate choices it entailed are revealed by what is surely the most remarkable story of his career. In 1959, fresh from his first detox treatment in Lexington, Kentucky, Don was arrested again and sentenced to five years in prison at Cheshire for violation of probation. "I'm beating this thing," he said to himself.

> I read a book on mental breakdowns. I figured that if a guy cut his wrists to get out of that cell, *that* they could handle. But if I just acted like a guy who wanted to do his time and not hurt himself, all the while planting seeds on them that would make *them* come and tell *me* I was sick — then I'd be reversing the psych on them. Meanwhile, I found out that a new psychiatrist was coming in that month. I knew that was my chance —to hit that guy on his first day there, while he was still confused, before he was broken into the jailhouse shit.
>
> From my reading I decided to build up a foundation for paranoia. When the guards came by my cell late at night, I'd say these little things to them, especially the ones that were amateur psychologists. I set those dudes right up. Then, the day the doctor came in, I went into a catatonic thing. I decided on that because I didn't know that much

about what I was doing — it was a tricky thing I was getting into — and I thought if I talked I might say something wrong and blow it. I only had one shot to make it out of there, you know; if they caught me bullshitting they'd never believe me again. But if I didn't talk, the doctor wouldn't be able to say that there was nothing wrong with me. He couldn't speculate; he'd have to send me for observation and treatment.

I was in the shop making dyes on a machine, and I just froze, stared at this thing on the machine. The guards came around to see if they could get a reaction out of me. They made like they were shoving my hand in ice, but I had seen one of them turn on the hot water. It was lucky I did, because otherwise I would have jumped back and yelled. Funny, once I was prepared for the hot water I didn't really feel it. Then they brought me in to the doctor, and he went into his whole act — snapping his fingers, waving pencils. Right over his shoulder there was a spot on the venetian blind, and I looked dead at that spot. I just hypnotized myself — blocking everything out. That spot was all I saw. But I was listening as all the people I'd planted my seeds with — the guards, my boss — came around and put in their opinions. "He's really suspicious," they said. "Maybe he'd better change jobs." It was all paying off. So the doctor had to go along with them. I heard him say that they were sending me to Connecticut Valley Hospital in Middletown, and I was happy. I had made it.

While I was waiting for the car to take me to Middletown, a guard offered me a cigarette. He said, "Gee, I didn't know you were this bad. Can you talk to me?" I wanted that cigarette so bad; I wanted to say, "Yeah, give it to me"; but I figured I'd just have to carry this thing all the way, so I passed it up. Then they put me in the car with a *real* nut, and I did talk with him, because I knew they wouldn't care what *he* said about me.

Having "conned" his way into Middletown, he kept on conning once he got there.

I figured that if I could get the state to spend something like five thousand dollars on treatment for me, they would never put me back in a cell. So I worked up a paranoid act by thinking back to some paranoid people I'd come across at Norwich State Hospital. I began hearing voices from Cheshire — people were calling me, people were trying to poison me, and so forth. I went to town on the Rorschach test; I saw my next-door neighbor in it, I saw everybody I knew. I said I hadn't reported to my probation officer because he was against me, always chasing me around. I wanted to make them think I was sick before I ever came to Cheshire, before I committed that parole violation. I got a psychologist who was fresh out of school, and I had him eating out of my hand.

The staff was just covering their ass, and I was manipulating that reaction, using them. I was bucking for insulin shock therapy. I worked it into my paranoid fantasies. I said that the people who were chasing me were trying to give me some treatment, something to do with insulin. What I was doing was planting seeds. I wanted them to think that they had considered giving me insulin therapy at Norwich, because this would give them the idea of doing it themselves. Sure enough, they asked me where I had heard about insulin. I said, "Oh, I don't know. I don't need any treatment now. When can I go back to Cheshire?" "Oh, Mr. Flanagan," they said, "don't you worry about going back there."

When he devised his "bug act" at Cheshire, Don had faced two bad choices — self-inflicted pain versus five years in the penitentiary. It is not only the heroin addict who faces such choices. As Lee points out, "Women who are locked into bad marriages have two bad choices — to stay with the marriage or get out. Most of the time they stay." The physical pain that Don chose simply dramatizes the dilemmas that occur in all of our lives. Don decided that having his hand held in scalding water was the better of two bad choices. He made the same choice again when he underwent insulin shock therapy.

> I almost copped out when I saw what insulin treatment is like. They put you down on a bed and give you insulin, and you go to sleep for five hours. During those hours you go through a lot of changes; you kick and thrash and then go into a third-stage coma. It's so serene — it clears out the cobwebs. But that first part — when I saw that line of people kicking around on those beds, I thought, "This ain't worth it." Then I said to myself, "I've come this far, I might as well go through with it. It can't kill me, I hope."

Don kept up his act to the end. Placed on an open ward with women in the next room, he restrained himself from being too forward in the dayroom.

> I did meet some interesting people there that I could talk to, but I never let on to anybody that I was gaming. This was too important to have anybody blow it for me, and I didn't trust anyone. As much as I wanted to say to somebody, "You know, you're all a bunch of fools, man," I kept it in. I planned it all out and stuck to it.

Don spent five months in prison before pulling his "bug act." Seven months later he was released from Connecticut Valley Hospital. Sentenced to five years, he spent but one in confinement. Later in those five years, in another prison, he had the bittersweet satisfaction of having a fellow inmate whom he had met in Cheshire ask him, "How's your brother up in Cheshire?" But in the immediate aftermath of his release he felt a quick comedown from the "high" of his accomplishment. Even on the outside he couldn't tell anyone what he had done. "Nobody would believe me — and I was afraid of being sent back." And now he just had to face life again. His arrest record disqualified him for most jobs, and when he did get a job he could keep it only as long as he kept his connection.

> When my connection was cut off I didn't have the drug at hand to let me go to work every day. So I had to start running for the drug again, and running meant missing work. The job became secondary, and after a while I was just running for the drug.

Don's unorthodox prison breakout reflected his consistent preference for the medical as opposed to the criminal model of drug addiction. He wanted to be treated as a "sick," disabled person rather than accept responsibility for having broken the law. More than that, he chose to present himself to the world as a disabled person rather than accept the normal responsibilities of living. If Don did not have teachers of responsibility in his youth, neither did he have them (by his own account) in the institutions in which he spent much of his young adulthood — even the more benign institutions like Lexington:

> Lexington offered supervised withdrawal, abstinence from drugs, and a health kick — three good meals a day, regular sleep, and good healthy farm work. That was okay so far as it went. On the other hand, it gave me a lot of names, a lot of connections, because I met people there from all over the country who used drugs. And it was a protected existence; it didn't have much to do with the life I would have to adjust to on the outside. At

> Lexington, I didn't have to take any responsibilities for myself, so how was I being prepared to exercise responsibility later?

The job discrimination Don faced was real, but as he got deeper into his addiction he actually anticipated and deliberately invoked such disqualification in a way that recalls Winick's analysis of adolescent heroin use as a strategy for remaining dependent on others (and on institutions). When on occasion he was offered a job by someone who saw what a good talker he was, he simply revealed that he was, regrettably, a victim of the dread disease of drug addiction. He was quite capable of saying to a shocked loan company representative on the telephone, "I'll be down to pick up the loan, but I have more important business to attend to first. I have to shoot up." He volunteered the information, he now says. "because I couldn't handle that sort of burden, and I needed an out."

There was another kind of burden that he couldn't handle. In the hospital at Middletown he met a woman from a well-to-do family who had had a breakdown. Once out of the hospital they started going together. For several weeks Don surprised himself and played it straight.

> Then I ran into a guy who gave me ten bags to get rid of, and I took them because I needed a little extra money. I went to New Haven, put the bags in a hotel room, and went out with this girlfriend to see Tennessee Williams' *Sweet Bird of Youth.* And all the while my mouth was watering for that bag of dope; I forgot all about the woman. Afterward I took her home right away, went back to my hotel, dropped the bag in the cooker, and got off.

"She wanted me to be the strong one, to take the lead," he reflects. "I was afraid of it -- afraid of the responsibility." He implies that he took drugs again partly to get out of the relationship, just as he had quit school to get away from another girlfriend who expected too much of him. Here was a man who welcomed and called down upon himself the disabling image of the heroin addict.

The life Don chose to return to at times like this (for in it, hard grind though it was, he found some security and comfort) was that described by Edward Preble and John Casey in an article called "Taking Care of Business: The Heroin User's Life on the Street."[2] Here is Don telling how he "nodded away years of my life:"

> This was what an average day was like for me. I'd get up, go to the bathroom, and get some water for my morning wake-up. I'd empty the bag into a bottle cap and cook the thing up, thinking of nothing but the excitement of getting the stuff into me. Then I'd draw it up and take the hit. I'd sit for just a minute or so to feel it coming on. It would take away the aches and pains that were starting to come at me. Then I'd get busy organizing my day. I'd have to make fifty or sixty bucks -- more in later years -- to get enough stuff to last till the next morning. It got to the point where the heroin straightened me out just enough so I could function when I hustled for the next shot.

He and his friends made most of their money by "boosting" items from stores and immediately returning them for a refund. One of them would "lift" the item and take it out to a waiting car, where his partner would put it in a store bag and take it back in. "My wife just bought me this," he would tell the clerk, "and it seems I already have one." This was easy to do back in the fifties, when there was more trust around to abuse. Later, in the era of receipts and uniformed guards, it still could be done, but it required a greater effort to intimidate a clerk.

It wasn't only among storekeepers that there was a decline of trust. As time went on Don observed a growing paranoia in himself and his companions.

> Slowly but surely, your value system deteriorates. You say, "I will never steal," but then you feel the pressures, and you go under. First you may say you'll let someone else do the shoplifting while you wait outside in the car. Three weeks later you're in that store with the guy because you don't want him to beat you out of anything.

The deterioration he speaks of, physical as well as ethical, was to become more and more pronounced.

* * *

Alcoholism, too, has its three stages. The second stage typically can be recognized by such signs as loss of control, extravagance, aggression, conflicts with family and friends, business setbacks, periods of abstinence, and attempts at treatment. By the time Lee moved to Florida he was well into a full-blown addiction. Realizing how serious his "problem" had become, he stayed away from liquor until one night in Miami wnen he went out on the town with his secretary's sister.

> The police picked me up at three A.M. driving down the sidewalk. I was laughing. I figured it was like back in Manchester -- what could anybody do to me? What a fight I put up when I realized that they were actually booking me and throwing me in jail. "You can't do this to me!" I screamed at them. "Don't you know who I am? I'm a respectable businessman, a regular guy. I'm not some common drunk!"

This is the way many alcoholics feel the first time they see the inside of a jail or a hospital. Later, when they've been back again and again, they get to thinking, "Maybe this is where I belong. Maybe I *am* a common drunk." It happened that way to Lee in hospitals, but not in prisons. There were afternoons when he would stagger out of the bar in one Hilton or another and look across the street at the drunks in the park. What separated him from them was the money and connections that they weren't fortunate enough to have.

This incident in Miami was the only time Lee ever heard a cell door close behind him, and the experience had as much impact on him as anything could have had at that time.

> When I woke up and realized where I was -- locked in a cell in a place where I didn't know anybody, where there was nobody I could call for help -- I felt alone and ashamed and remorseful like never before. I said to myself, "Lee, you've done a lot of rotten things, but this is the lowest." I made a bargain with God that if I ever got out of that jail, it would be straight and narrow from then on. I'll never forget that feeling. It kept me from drinking for hours.

It turned out to be more like "back in Manchester" than Lee had figured. Suddenly remembering some local "connections," he had a judge paid off and was immediately released.

Back together with Doris after their six-week separation, Lee brought his family down to Florida and opened a new branch of the insurance business, leaving his partner to manage the Connecticut branch. Again the successes started rolling in. Again Lee "told myself it had to be luck. Because it couldn't be me." Again he started drinking.

Lee lived in Florida from 1959 to 1964. It was there that he drove an hour and a half to Fort Myers to see an alcoholic who had written a book claiming that a Vitamin B formula could kill the desire for drink -- and then started taking vitamin pills with his liquor. Lee would go any distance, spend any amount of money to try to find a magical answer that would enable him to control his drinking (but not stop it). Wherever such a solution was advertised -- something that would let him have the pleasure without the pain -- there Lee was to be found.

It was in Florida, too, that he had his one and only physical altercation with Doris. Afterward he blacked out and didn't remember having hit her. To this day, though, he remembers it whenever he looks at the scars on his leg. While swinging at Doris he fell onto the bed and cut his leg. In the overwrought state that both he and Doris were in, neither of them did anything about getting the wounds stitched. So in their one brawl it was Lee who got the worst of it.

The incident prompted these memorable reflections:

> That was a level I'd sworn I'd never reach. But then I had also sworn once that I would never touch a drink because of what I'd seen it do to people. One by one I was breaking those vows. It's a game we play with ourselves: "I'll never go to jail," and I wound up in jail; "I'll never leave my family," and I left them; "I'll never smash up a car," and I smashed several of them; "I'll never hit my wife," and I hit her. Each thing I would justify by saying it would never happen again. But then I'd do something else. Each time I'd think, "How far down can you go?" But I found out you can go a lot farther down.

Whenever Lee did something destructive, particularly something that threatened his marriage, he showed a lot of remorse and made amends with gestures like seeing a psychiatrist or going "dry" for a while. Always he was sorry; always he promised, "I'll never do *that* again!" -- until the next time. For he didn't stop drinking. He couldn't stop. He panicked at the thought. It would have been "like choking off my own air supply."

> I've seen people who really want a cigarette when it's midnight and there's no place to buy a pack. They're like rats trapped in a corner; they run out and try to find cigarette butts on the street that they can smoke. I've seen people go into a physical panic when they get put down by a lover. That's how it was with me when I didn't lay in a

> Sunday supply of booze. That's how it was one Thanksgiving evening when I was temporarily grounded in Wichita, Kansas, where there was no liquor. I felt like I was drowning.

To ward off this menacing prospect, Lee lived a life that can only be called monomaniacal. It was a life totally governed by alcohol. Wherever he was, whatever he was doing, Lee was always racing from one drink to the next while at the same time covering his tracks. He set up each of his various environments both to guarantee his liquor supply and to provide him with "cover stories" for the people he associated with. His living arrangements and travel arrangements revolved around his liquor arrangements. These were the living skills he developed so that he could have the life he wanted. When he traveled by plane, for example,

> I'd get to the airport two hours early (oh, my strict punctuality, I'd tell people) so I could spend that time in the bar, and I'd be flying before I ever got on the plane. On the plane I'd be drinking the two drinks the stewardess gave out, plus something from the bottle I carried in the compartment I had sewn into my suit pockets or my briefcase. If the plane made a stop for ten minutes, I'd be calculating how much time I had to race to the bar and back (always with the excuse of having to make a phone call or buy a paper) and how many drinks I could have in that time. Back on the plane, I might luck out and have a new stewardess who would qualify me for two more drinks. If not, I could always turn to the person next to me and say, "Excuse me, I see you're not ordering the two drinks you're entitled to. You know, I don't usually drink this way, but my mother's deathly ill, my nerves are shot....You know these crazy regulations; would you mind ordering your two drinks for me?" I'd lie and I'd cry to get those extra drinks because I had no pride left.

At restaurants:

> I'd pick a place with a separate bar that was near the men's room, so I'd have an excuse to run off for some quickies. I'd go to the men's room, all right -- to drink the shot I'd picked up at the bar on the way. Coming back to the table, I'd gulp a second drink at the bar. I'd let the people who were with me think I had a weak bladder. Then they'd wonder why I passed out after supposedly sipping one drink with them.
>
> Sometimes I did need that men's room. How many nights I'd eat like a pig (when I was eating at all), excuse myself from the table, and throw up the whole dinner. Then I'd wash my face, take a breath freshener, come back to the table, and start again as if nothing had happened.

In motels:

> I always got a room next to the ice machine. I turned on the television before anything else, because I needed to have those voices going -- I couldn't stand being alone. I'd have it all set up, the TV and my bar, and the next morning I'd wake up first with vomiting, then dry heaves, hugging the toilet bowl. Great fun, wasn't it? That was really living. Sometimes I couldn't brush my teeth without choking, so I learned the technique of sitting there and brushing one tooth at a time. And sometimes, if I'd blacked out the night before, I'd have to call the switchboard and ask a lot of devious leading questions or else check the inscription on the Bible or the stationery to find out what city I was in. But the switchboard or the Bible couldn't tell me how I got there. Somehow I lost a day, a night, a city. Any of you "normal" people ever misplace a city?

And, finally, at home:

> I used to rationalize to shrinks that my biggest problem was drinking on weekends; if only I could find some way to occupy those Saturdays and Sundays. Other guys have hobbies like watching football and playing cards -- you know, hobbies that put wives and children through the kind of anguish that alcoholism does. My hobby was drinking. Holidays were the same. I'd celebrate Christmas like nobody ever had. It was my way of forgetting those sad Christmases I had as a kid. Everybody loves one another at Christmas time, and I just drank and drank so I could stay in that eternal state of love. But at the height of the party a chill would come over me. "My God, Lee," I'd say, "what do you do when they all go home? What do you do when the music stops?" What would I do when the drinking was over and I'd be lying in bed with nobody there and wake up at three in the morning with that terrifying feeling?

Lee did a lot of "rationalizing to shrinks" in his days of active alcoholism. He told them what they expected to hear, and they told him what he wanted to hear. "I'm perfectly willing to give up alcohol," he would say. "No, you don't have to. You just have to control it. There's nothing wrong with a couple of drinks," the shrink would tell him. "Sure, if you say so," he would reply. Lee now thinks that the psychiatrists he saw when he was drinking didn't do him any good because they were either too psychoanalytic or too non-directive and uninvolved. "Lee," one of them would say, "how can we get to your *real* problems when you come in here bombed or hung over?" By not confronting him with the fact that his drinking itself was the problem, these well-intentioned doctors only reinforced Lee's denial system.

In Florida one psychiatrist did help Lee cut down his drinking by introducing him to another addiction -- tranquilizers. She gave him an open-ended prescription for Librium, which raised him to new "highs" in combination with smaller amounts of alcohol. The pills calmed his stomach in the morning and enabled him to drink without getting sick so much. Maybe this was the magic that would give him the pleasure of drinking without the pain, the "high" without the hassle.

As the pace of Lee's business activity intensified, however, so did his consumption of both the pills and alcohol. Fortified by legitimate doctors with bottles of a thousand, he was popping five 25-milligram pills of Librium four times a day, plus Seconals and sleeping pills at night -- on top of the booze. He went for long periods without eating, punctuated by bouts of ravenous hunger. He lost the capacity to sleep except when drugged or when he passed out from drinking. And the pills affected his memory, so that he would get up at night and take handfuls at a time without knowing how many he had taken the time before. Yet somehow his survival instinct, combined with a little luck, operated to keep him from overdosing on the potentially lethal mix of barbiturates and alcohol. Today Lee considers himself fortunate not to have suffered any permanent impairment to his health, such as brain damage, from the drinking and the pills.

At the time, though, he suffered numerous breakdowns and hospitalizations -- "a weekend here, a few days there" -- during as well as after the period in which he took the pills. During the first of these he was kept on a locked ward except when his three young children came to visit. He was ashamed that they should see him that way. Yet within months he was so accustomed to the routine that he was joking with the chronic patients and calling the orderlies by name.

Meanwhile, in a fit of grandiose bad judgment, Lee sold his insurance partnership after eight successful years. "The more people advised me not to sell," he recalls, "the more I set myself to do it, just like when people told me not to get married. When I was drinking, there was no greater industrialist and financier. Henry Ford, watch out!"

At the same time, just as with the woman he *didn't* marry, Lee was running from confrontation. He sold the business because he believed that his partner wasn't dealing with him honestly.

Rather than face the immediate discomfort of standing up for his rights, he did what was easy in the short run, but harmful in the long run. "That was my Charlie Brown solution: 'No problem is so big or small that I can't run away from it.'" Then, too, there was always the hope that selling the business would change his life. Moving to Florida hadn't worked, but maybe that was just the wrong escape hatch.

When President Kennedy was assassinated Lee sat around drinking and crying all weekend. He was mourning partly for Kennedy, partly for himself. It was the beginning of a binge that lasted a month. During the Christmas holidays Lee got up one morning and was unable to sign his name to a check. He knew what his name was, but he couldn't coordinate his hand with his mind. It was scary. Alcohol by itself had never made him feel *that* crazy, that much out of control.

He went into the hospital for thirty days' observation on the psychiatric ward. There he was given the "socially acceptable" diagnosis (which his wife was only too happy to hear) of a mental breakdown or "anxiety reaction" — anything but alcoholism. During that month in the hospital he gave up the pills for good. It was either that or the liquor.

> I hadn't slept without pills since I was eighteen years old. *That* was addiction. I went twenty nights without sleeping, playing double solitaire with the nurses all night long and catching an hour's sleep here and there during the day. Alcohol withdrawal was never like that.
>
> I never went back on the pills. I kept large supplies, though, until I finally threw them out two years after I became sober, which was eight years after I stopped taking the pills. I counted 2500 pills that I kept in my house all those years, like a security blanket.

He came out dry and depressed. Sometimes he would sit with his therapist for forty-five minutes without either of them saying a word. Just as Don realized after he beat his prison sentence that he had no other life to go back to except that of a drug user, Lee saw that he couldn't live without alcohol. "Couldn't work, couldn't study, couldn't sell, couldn't socialize, couldn't listen to jazz, couldn't watch TV, couldn't have sex — without booze." He wouldn't give up something that made him feel good (at least superficially) for nothing, no alternatives, only continued bad feelings. So when he was offered a temporary job as a traveling consultant with an expense account, he jumped at the invitation to drink again.

> I had trained myself, as many alcoholics do, to do my work very effectively in a very short time. Be fast and thorough, and then you're free to drink. And at this point in my life I had given up. I didn't care what sleazy bar I was in or who I was with. I hooked up with anybody.

***

When Jerry returned to the Bronx in 1956, he entered into the street life and took up the addict's daily grind that Don has described. "In terms of energy," he says, "it was much like what I do now -- getting up at six, not coming home until eleven, driving two hundred miles a day to teach in different parts of the state." Jerry and his friend Irving were "sneak thieves -- like a guy jumping a fence, taking a chicken, and running down the road with it as fast as he can." Chickens were nowhere to be had in the Bronx, but there were plenty of momentarily unoccupied apartments that Jerry and Irving could break into and take cash, jewelry, radios, silverware -- whatever they could carry off without having a car. That did not include television sets, which were not yet portable. But if there were fewer TVs in the Bronx in those days, there were a lot more open windows than there are now. It was easy stuff; it was also small-time stuff. So Jerry and his friends would also cash stolen welfare checks or venture downtown to Macy's or Gimbel's, where they practiced the shoplift-for-refund game that Don mastered in Hartford.

From time to time Jerry was bused for these crimes or for

possession of works (needle, eye-dropper, and spoon or cap). Sometimes he was let go; sometimes he did a "skid bit" (thirty-day stretch) in a local prison like Riker's Island. When he wasn't in jail he lived with his mother. It was ironic that Jerry, who had been out on his own when he was seven or eight, was living with his mother at twenty-one.

> My mother sensed that something was wrong in my life, but she didn't want to know about it. She was too involved in her own world to confront me about mine. When I was in jail she sent me letters, but she didn't visit me, and I didn't ask her to come. My mother and I had an accommodation with each other. She no doubt felt guilty about not having given me a home when I was a child, so as long as I didn't hassle her too much, she let me be. For my part, I realized that it was between living with her and living on a roof or in the basement of a shooting gallery somewhere. She gave me a couch, and I didn't need much more. I, too, was very busy from early morning till late at night. I was out burglarizing and stealing, making my connection, and then perhaps watching a ball game or a movie or trying to work up some sexual activity with one of the ladies in my peer group.

The group that Jerry was a part of defined itself aggressively by its allegiance to heroin. With the sense of shared "turf" that is described in *Love and Addiction* as well as in *Drugs Don't Take People; People Take Drugs,*[3] these heroin users looked contemptuously upon those who smoked marijuana. "Get that shit out of here," they would say. "What do you want to do -- smoke grass or get high?" It was like the horror expressed by the socially respectable alcoholic at the crimes committed by heroin addicts. Throughout his days as an addict Jerry never thought it worth the effort to get high on anything but heroin. Nothing else was quite real.

Jerry enjoyed the fun and camaraderie for a year and a half

after his return to New York. He was regarded as a "nuts and bolts" or "meat and potatoes" man -- something in between a real hustler and a beggar or hanger-on. Then, at the beginning of 1958, his career took a different turn from Don's. His supplier, who saw Jerry as a "responsible guy" within the definitions of the street world, recruited him to sell dope, something Don never did except in the most incidental ways.

> I started small with half-loads, which were three-dollar bags. I would buy them for ten dollars a piece and sell for thirty, splitting the profit with my supplier. Since he was already tapping his bag and I wasn't, it quickly became known that I had a good bag. People came looking for Jerry's bag, and I started putting red scotch tape on my bags to identify them.
>
> Dealing was a real step up for me. I could sleep later in the morning and still supply my habit with all the dope I wanted to shoot, yet I had enough discipline not to shoot up all the profits. I was making a lot of money, and I enjoyed the attentions of several female addicts who would do sexual favors for drugs. Eventually I moved out of my mother's apartment to live with one of these women.
>
> The bad side was that I wasn't having so much fun any more. Instead of camaraderie I was feeling pressure. I was becoming a more familiar figure in the neighborhood -- which, as I said, was no longer exclusively Jewish. I became a target for addicts who wanted to hold me up for dope and money. I also became a target for law enforcement agencies, who continually shook me down because they knew I was a dealer, though I was smart enough not to carry any with me. I began to have the feeling that there wasn't enough of me to give to everyone who wanted me. With all that pressure I started using more dope

> than ever before. Sometimes I was getting off three to five times a day. To supply my habit and my girlfriend's I started tapping the bags, taking one-third for myself, before I put them out on the street.

The morality of dealing was not an issue for Jerry. As he rightly says,

> I didn't have to take out classified ads to sell my wares. The "pusher" who hung around schoolyards peddling drugs was a myth. That just didn't happen; there was no need for it. The demand was too much for the supply. I never looked to give people their wings -- that is, introduce them to drugs. And I didn't sell to kids. On the other hand, when I had people dealing for me I didn't tell them to check anybody's ID.

There was, however, another kind of morality that drove him on to excel as a dealer. The community he lived in was achievement-oriented. "People were always working, doing things. It was important to be successful at whatever you did. So to me it was important to be a good burglar, a good dope seller, to be of good standing in my part of the community." Although Jerry shared Don's educational disadvantages, as he rose in the drug-dealing network he became, in his own way, a successful Jewish businessman like Lee.

> When I got to be dealing ten, twenty, thirty half-loads a day, I was introduced to my supplier's Italian wholesalers in the East Bronx. Later my supplier was busted and sent away for a long time. The Italians, seeing me as a good source in the neighborhood, suggested that I get off the front line and do some recruiting myself. I then had three or four people dealing for me on the street. I was making more money than ever -- close to two hundred dollars a day, of which I would shoot up about seventy or eighty -- and

> getting lots of strokes from my wholesalers. For the first time I was venturing far out of my community to pick up the dope, and there were amounts of money being exchanged -- hundreds, sometimes thousands of dollars -- that I had never seen before.
>
> My life became more hectic. With some trustworthy junkies I would take a vast sum of money across town in a cab, pick up the dope, and bring it back. Next, I started dealing in ounces instead of in bags. I learned the ritual of cutting the dope myself. I had to have the heroin, the quinine, the milk sugar -- everything in proper proportion -- and a mirror or a glass to put it in. I spent hours bagging up because I wouldn't trust anyone else to do it, until the business got so big that I had to. I got two women and my old friend Irving to do it, and I watched them as a mother watches her babes. I wouldn't blink an eye.

The sharp eye for verbal and non-verbal behavior that Jerry developed in this kind of transaction was later to serve him well when he put such living skills to different uses as a counselor and teacher. At this point, however, no amount of skill in sizing people up could keep him out of hot water. He was coming into contact with more and more people that he didn't know, and things were getting out of control. A bust was inevitable.

By the fall of 1958 Jerry had aged considerably during ten months of dealing. "I now look back on those ten months," he says, "as one of the heaviest periods in my life." Eventually he made some sales to a person who turned out to be a federal narcotics agent and was arrested.

> I was scared of the time I was facing. At sixteen, when I was sent to Elmira, I had nothing. Here I had a clientele, a girlfriend, new clothes, a car -- some stature. I didn't want to go. But my Italian connections (who had put up my bail) told me,

> "Do your time. There's always something for you when you get back." They didn't make any threats, but I knew what would happen to me if I cooperated with the federal authorities. However, I hadn't for a moment considered cooperating.

Under a recently enacted law, since Jerry was under twenty-five he was sentenced as a youthful (as distinct from juvenile) offender to a zero-to-six-year term, during which he could be released at the discretion of the government. In a federal detention center in New York he kicked the biggest habit he ever had "with some discomfort, but I never climbed walls or thought of hanging myself. It was a thing we called 'the chucks,' and it typically left one very hungry, ravenous."

He was then sent to a federal reformatory in Chillicothe, Ohio.

> As with Elmira, I have a warm memory of Chillicothe, where I was exposed to kids from all the great cities. I really learned how to do time there. I was completely involved in reformatory life. Having learned to type in the service, I became a clerk in the recreation department as well as for the Catholic priest. I was coaching the softball team, managing the basketball team, winning cigarettes (even from the guards) in football pools, playing cards, running for cookies at the commissary, stealing fried chicken from the officers' mess. It was a lot of fun. A kind of deference was paid me because I had been a big dealer in New York, and whenever somebody sneaked some dope in, I always got my nose into it. I was the Jack Anderson of Chillicothe. I knew what was happening all the time.
>
> I had one tense moment in Chillicothe. While I was coming out of the shower, a big white kid from the Midwest patted me on my ass. I knew what that meant. I had to do something -- but

> what? Ignore it and hope he wouldn't do it again? Tell the guards and have them intervene? That wouldn't do any good. Fight on the spot? I'd get beaten up and ripped off. So instead, I busted him over the head with my tray in the chow hall. I knew that to keep order in such a large assemblage, the guards would have to break it up before there could be much of a fight. I showed the guy that I might be small, but I was not to be trifled with. He later made friends with me and became my bodyguard while I was dealing.

Inside prison walls as well as outside, the con man was playing a winning game. Here again Jerry's career can be contrasted with Don's. Whenever Don was arrested he would seek to have himself transferred to a hospital or treatment facility, where he would develop symptoms that enabled him to bargain with doctors for psychotropic medications. If he could not get drugs prescribed for him, he got by without drugs because the institution spared him from having to expend much energy in managing his life. Jerry, on the other hand, simply reconciled himself to the fact that he was not going to get high while he was incarcerated (except occasionally when drugs were smuggled in). To him and his friends, "high" meant heroin, and he was not going to get that from doctors.

To a degree the two men's different approaches to drugs reflected local customs and attitudes. In Connecticut it was common for addicts to steal cough medicine from drug stores and use the codeine as a substitute for heroin. This was not done in Jerry's New York milieu. But there was plenty of opportunity to get into dope dealing in Connecticut as well as in New York, and Don did not do so. Outside as well as inside institutions, Don did not choose the active life that Jerry did.

What is so remarkable about Jerry is that he lived with the same zest, productivity, and apparent happiness when he was off drugs as when he was on. In part this was a reflection of the achievement orientation which he shared with Lee. Like Lee, Jerry was later to marry and support children while he was feeding his addiction. When he was not in the business of dealing he had a legitimate salesman's job -- again like Lee. Beyond this (and here he differs from Lee as well as Don), Jerry didn't need drugs. He didn't need his morning shot, as Don has testified he did, to "take away the aches and pains that were starting to come at me" and help him organize his day. Jerry used heroin for self-definition and group identification, and he thrived under prison regimes that gave him these things without drugs. Since he wasn't driven by a constant need for the feeling the drug gave him, he had no reason to accept substitutes, as Don accepted codeine, Dilaudid, or tranquilizers, or as Lee, after telling himself that he would never touch some cheap liquors, would drink whatever he could get if no other source of alcohol was at hand.

Going by Jerry's account of himself, one might wonder why he wanted to get out of Chillicothe at all. Perhaps he was not as happy there as he says. There were, however, plausible enough reasons for him (like anyone else) to want out. The outside world offered women, movies, big-league ball games, and some personal freedom. Jerry had given up a lot when the authorities took him off the street. And if he didn't need to get high, he certainly liked it as much as he liked anything. Yet when he left prison it was with the intention of giving up that pleasure and all its associations.

> After two and a half years I made parole on the condition that I have a place to live. I gave my mother's address and smuggled out a letter asking her to tell the parole authorities that I would stay with her, though I promised her I really wouldn't. But she told them, "No matter what, he can't come here." Finally, after three years, I got out on the condition that I look for work.
>
> Here I was, twenty-six years old, currently on welfare, never having had a day's legal employment. I decided I wasn't going back on drugs, so I took an apartment in another section of the Bronx. I was really afraid of going back to the old neighborhood.

Jerry saw that dealing, which had given him all the things he had had before going to jail, had also put him in jail. He didn't want to go back to Chillicothe, so he didn't go back and ask his Italian contacts to set him up again. Instead, he took a job selling ladies' shoes and accessories at A.S. Beck during the Christmas season.

> I liked it; it was another hustle to sell those shoes and handbags and polish for a commission. I did so well that I was the only person asked to stay on after Christmas. I got recognition, praise, and a decent salary, and for a while that made me happy. I began to question what I had been doing up to that point. I was reading more, meeting different types of people, but mainly I think it was TV. I would watch the same programs over and over again -- *The Roaring Twenties, Hong Kong, Hawaiian Eye.* I'd see guys who didn't look much smarter than I was, and yet they had the girls, the cars, the money, the respect. What did I have if I was so smart? But it was just too painful, and I discounted it.

When Jerry turned back to his old life, it was not (he says) because he felt miserable without drugs, but because his new life didn't make him feel good enough.

> Measured against the active life I had led in Chillicothe and before, against the amount of daily stimulation I found natural, the life I had now couldn't sustain me. I lived alone, and all I did was come home and look at a used TV. I had no support system except an overloaded parole officer who would say, "You working? Okay. See you in a month." The only satisfaction I had was in my job. And after abut four months that, too, became boring when I found I could excel at it without much effort.
>
> "Let me go back to the neighborhood," I

thought, "and see what the fellas are doing."

* * *

"The drug started to dominate when it became the end in itself, when I lost interest in the things the drug had helped me appreciate." In this one lucid sentence Don summarizes how the addictive involvement destroys every other focus of an already weakened life. Lee first drank for the sake of doing business, then did business for the sake of drinking. Even Jerry speaks of his hustling and dealing as having turned into work instead of fun.

But the seeds of these outcomes were all there before drugs or alcohol ever entered the picture. From the beginning, Don and Lee were driven by fear. The paradox of manipulativeness and passivity in these talented individuals is striking. Both could do audacious, imaginative things -- Lee the "con man," Don with the "bug act" that got him out of jail. Yet Lee at the end could sit in a bar watching his business fall apart, and Don could sit in an institution watching his whole life go by. When Don stood before a judge and played the role of an innocent youth, or when he adopted the "sick role" to get himself transferred from jail to hospital, he was indeed manipulating the authorities, but he was also acting out a parody of what he really was.
also acting out a parody of what he really was.

The externality -- the unreal quality -- of Lee's and Don's experience carried over strongly from their youth through their years of addiction. Nowhere was this falseness more apparent, and nowhere were the contradictions in their lives more persistent, than in their relationships with people. Since addiction commonly has its origins in an unease with oneself, it is not surprising that Lee, for example, couldn't bear to be alone, to the point where he had to turn to the TV in a motel room for companionship. But addiction is intrinsically a state of aloneness. Don felt that he had no personal relationships, no social identity -- a condition which was both a cause and a result of his drug use. What did President Kennedy's death have to do with him, he asks:

> His life didn't have any connection with mine. I wasn't a part of society. No mail ever came; nobody ever sent me a bill. I think I could have dropped dead, and nobody but my mother would have known the difference.

Even when there isn't this extreme anonymity, an addict's relationships with people tend to be hopelessly compromised, both by the demands of the addiction and by the emotional brittleness that led up to it. It is as if an addict's relationship with the rest of the world, and the relationships among addicts themselves, take the form of a perverse mirror-image of the interpersonal deprivations of the child the addict once was.

The addict's dealings with almost everyone outside the drug-using circle are frankly manipulative. Don admits that he "hooked up with all kinds of people who were out for an easy buck -- prostitutes, alcoholics, anyone who had a hustle." Consider Don's and Lee's characteristic cynicism about doctors. "I could make doctors think just what I wanted them to think," Don exults. "Doctors want a quick diagnosis, so you just have to act consistent for a month, and you've got them." Lee concurs. "If you want sleeping pills," he advises, "just tell the doctor you're not sleeping too well. That way you're letting him know what he can do for you, but you're not taking the responsibility of asking."

But what about human contacts within the addict circle? Don and Lee quite honestly report that these, too, are shallow and exploitive. Addicts steal from each other whenever they have to -- or maybe whenever they get a chance to. Don knows well what would happen when his back was turned.

> Once when I went to jail some people I called friends invaded my house and told my mother they were looking for something they had given me. Then they ransacked the place. They went through every drawer and every suit I had for a few bags or a set of works. They were vultures, just like me. I've done the same things in other people's houses, like raiding medicine cabinets.

They share with each other, in Don's words, "only the superficial feelings. We would rap, dream, listen to music, talk about how great the high was." But nothing about emotional needs, about inner vulnerability. Lee says the same about his drinking buddies. "I could be comfortable with them, but I couldn't talk about my feelings. They wouldn't understand, I felt. 'If they really knew me,' I felt, 'they wouldn't like me.'" Don captures this alienation and mutual self-deception in the following reminiscence:

> After a while I got to feel pretty detached from the people I was hustling and shooting up with. I didn't identify with them because they weren't going through the same things I was -- or if they were, they didn't let on. I knew it didn't feel so hot any more, but you wouldn't know that from the way we talked to each other. The only feeling we shared was the high.

In Don's relationships with women addicts we can hear a haunting echo of his early years with his mother.

> I realized what a lonely life it was when I was finishing up a jail term or criminal commitment with guys who had wives waiting for them to come out. I had nobody. When I had a relationship, it was with somebody who was using drugs, too. And it wasn't really a relationship; we had a common ground, but we'd beat each other in a second. She'd beat me for my stuff and I'd beat her for hers, though as long as we had some stuff together we could relax and share some things. Sometimes when I'd get away to some nice place like the Public Garden in Boston and see couples who appeared to be enjoying themselves without chemicals, people who were laughing and smiling and happy, I used to feel lonely and wonder what was wrong. Why couldn't I have that?

Don's reflections bring us to the all-important theme of the addict group: its reality, its power, its hollowness. It is truly a group of loners. Don's most telling point comes when he recognizes that the group's identity, and its members' involvement with each other, is based on one thing only:

> While we were using drugs together I identified with them. Once they stopped we had nothing more in common. I didn't know who these people were when they weren't using drugs; I didn't want to understand who they were becoming. I probably resented the fact that they had found the strength to get along without drugs. And if that was how I had reacted then, I knew that was how others would feel about me if I stopped using.

It is only natural that a group made up of refugees from human society will reflect, in its own inner workings, the collective incompleteness and insecurity of its members -- individuals who have never been shown what it is like to have integrity in a relationship.

Yet the group, for all its one-dimensional impersonality, is vital to the addict. It is all he has to bolster him against a disapproving world. When Don got in trouble with the law he was careful never to implicate anyone else, so that he could be "secure in my relationship with the guys I was involved with." Jerry did the same. In Elmira Reformatory, he says, "I had a group I could identify with that liked me and appreciated my skills. When had I ever had anything better?" Starting so often from a position of aloneness, a lack of real family and friends, the addict is on a lifelong journey in search of social support. He is looking for people who will confirm him in being what he is. The drug-using peer group is a first step -- sometimes the only step he will ever take -- in that search.

Still, his identification with the group tends to be equivocal. Lee understands this very well when he recalls his own two-sided attitude toward the world of the "squares:"

> All I could feel was self-pity. I thought I would never be able to reach out and touch what reality was like, to have life as life was supposed to be, because I was different: I was a boozer. Then I'd go to the other extreme of antagonism.

In that mood, he identified defensively with his fellow drinkers:

> Besides, I knew who the best people really were: my drinking buddies. I would walk into any bar, strike up a conversation, and feel right at home. Instant camaraderie. That was where the real people were.

From self-pity to antagonism: the outcast rejects the society that cast him out. Deviance becomes defiance as various groups, such as the users of different drugs, wear proudly the badges of their particular aberration, declaring themselves superior to the straight world as well as to each other, so that they can attach special meaning, special value to their desperate lives. When one gives up that deviance and leaves the group, one leaves it totally, henceforth to look upon it with an incomprehension and contempt that are returned in kind.

It is in this context that we can understand Jerry, who differs from Don and Lee in important ways. He did not regard his natural, unmedicated emotional state as one of pain and anguish. He did not suffer severe withdrawal anxiety. He did not deteriorate physically. He was able to live energetically and feel fulfilled when not using drugs, as in his enterprising prison career. He would claim, in fact (although this way of wording it is not his), that he was not really addicted to drugs *per se*.

Jerry's preoccupation with the drug "high" was never as great as Don's or Lee's. Rather, his behavior was shaped by his identification with a particular social group. Don, too, grew up in a tough neighborhood, and group membership did play a part in his becoming addicted. But while Don was somewhat alienated from and intimidated by the juvenile gangs he hung out with, Jerry had no such conflicts. He identified totally with his peers and participated wholeheartedly in their activities. Jerry's career, in contrast with Don's, suggests not so much an adolescent detour from responsibility as a continuation of childhood deviance and alienation from straight society. His story from this point on is really about the drawn-out process by which that identity was broken and replaced by another.

5
hitting bottom

Together with the humanistic educator Sidney Simon, who originated the idea, Lee has been working on a concept known as "systematic suicide," which explores (in a manner consistent with *Love and Addiction)* the continuum between dramatically self-destructive behavior and the things we do every day. We all know what suicide is. That's when someone drives a car off an embankment or into a tree at high speed (as Lee tried unsuccessfully to do) or puts a revolver to his temple. Systematic suicide is something different. It is when we take in a few more calories each day than we burn off. It is when we smoke cigarettes even though we know that they take, on the average, eleven years off a person's life. It is when we shorten our useful lives by sleeping ten hours a day or watching TV for five. Systematic suicide is progressive, step-by-step self-destruction, whether through drugs or alcohol, nicotine, poor stress management, lack of medical care, lack of exercise, the wrong kinds or amounts of food, inadequate work-leisure balance, not enough solitude, not enough contact with people, or anything else that creates a lack of proportion and lack of proper nourishment (physical, emotional, or spiritual). Any addiction that people can get locked into is a form of systematic suicide.

At this early stage in their thinking about systematic suicide, Lee and Sid Simon posit ten reasons why people engage in such self-destructive behavior.

First, people are endowed with an enormous capacity for magical thinking. Nobody starts out in life saying, "You know what? I think I'll become an alcoholic." "I'm going to become a junkie." "I intend to spend much of my life in jail." "I'm going to get fat." "I think it would be a nice idea to come down with lung cancer in twenty or thirty years." "I won't use seat belts so I can really get hurt if I have an accident." Instead, they think that somebody else will have the cancer or the fatal accident, that the fourth danish pastry won't show up on their waist line, that they can stop drinking or shooting up or overeating any time they want (as long as any time is tomorrow, not today). That's like believing in magic.

Second, people don't learn how to think critically. They don't see through the food ads, the liquor ads, the cigarette ads. They don't see through the hyped-up image of the "cool" drug user or the know-it-all down at the local bar. They don't know when they're being hustled.

Third, people feel that they don't deserve anything better than what they're getting. Someone who doesn't feel worthy is more likely to choose some form of self-inflicted injury than someone who feels that he or she deserves a good life.

Fourth, people have trouble identifying those things (including people and experiences) that they love. If they knew what was really important to them, they would build their lives around those things instead of being diverted by addictive escapes.

Fifth, people don't envision a clear future for themselves. The ability to plan for the future is regarded as a key sign of mental health. Counselors consider it vital to have potentially suicidal individuals commit themselves to some future action (such as making an appointment for another meeting). Making the future real is equally important in preventing systematic suicide. For if there is no clear future, why not eat, drink, and be merry? Tomorrow you may die — and if you go on living like that, one of these tomorrows you probably will.

Sixth, people don't believe they have enough to live for. Without positive alternatives, goals, hopes, involvements, people have little reason to take care of themselves, little reason to avoid the numbing comforts of addiction.

Seventh, people don't identify with others as role models. Instead of recognizing that others have the same feelings they do, people tell themselves, "It's easy for others to give up drinking (or whatever). It's easy for them to tell me to give it up. Nobody knows what a hard life I lead, what troubles I have." With an attitude like that, one locks oneself into a prison of self-pity and self-destructive behavior.

Eighth, people have poor intrapersonal skills. These include poor self-discipline and self-control, low frustration tolerance (Albert Ellis's term), and the inability to delay gratification. Such traits, of course, have long been associated with addiction and indeed largely define the addiction-prone personality.

Ninth, people have poor interpersonal skills. They are unable to communicate with others and to give and receive love. Addictions are sought as substitutes for love and communication — safe, reliable substitutes for living human connections that must be maintained by empathy and hard work.

Tenth, people don't accept responsibility for the consequences of their actions. "It's not my drinking that's the problem," they say. "It's my job, my marriage, the broken home I grew up in, the way people act toward me — all the things that have happened to me that *make* me drink." As Albert Ellis and William Glasser constantly stress, as long as people believe that they don't have the capacity to make choices, they will continue to make the same destructive choices they have made in the past.

Sidney Simon and Lee Silverstein currently are developing counseling methods to help people identify the forms of systematic suicide they are engaging in and do something about the ones they want to change (methods that are in line with *Consider the Alternative* and Simon's work in values clarification). The relevance of the idea of systematic suicide here is in connecting what seem like larger-than-life stories with the "normal" life we all live. In the third and last stage of addiction

Don, Lee and Jerry clearly were killing themselves. (We can include all three in this statement if we accept that a lifetime in jail is equivalent to death.) Now it was no longer a question of their taking drugs or alcohol to keep from getting sick. Now drugs and alcohol were *making* them sick — making it impossible for them either to live normally in society or to go on living at all. These are the most extreme, most visible, most concrete examples of systematic suicide one could imagine. Yet only with death or permanent institutionalization staring them in the face did Don, Lee, and Jerry change their behavior, and even then the issue was (and in one case again) in doubt. What about the rest of us, who tend to be much better insulated from the consequences of our actions? What about those of us whose addictions only make us a few pounds heavier each year, a little more tired or short of breath? What will it take to move us to change?

When someone is scared he'll do anything and promise still more. A driver who is stopped for speeding will drive very carefully for the next fifty miles or so and then gradually, imperceptibly, will begin to lean a little harder on the accelerator. Someone who is having an extramarital affair will at first take pains to go out to a motel in East Overshoes or Bigfoot; then, slowly, his guard comes down, and the errant lover is discovered a block away from home. When an alcoholic is confronted by his wife after he disrupts a family gathering, he will show remorse, abstain for a few weeks, go to a psychiatrist — until the next time he takes a drink and gets careless (or gets careless and takes a drink). A heroin addict who begins by hiding his works behind a block in the chimney may one day see them fall out of his pocket before his family's very eyes. "God, man, I've got to be more careful," he'll say to himself.

Don spent his last years as a heroin addict alternating between pleas of "Oh, yes, Your Honor, please, Your Honor, I'll do anything" (scenes similar to those Jerry staged 100 miles away) and a life of utter indifference and lassitude (the like of which Jerry would never know). Like Lee he gave up pill-taking after having a seizure, because "I knew I had a good mind and didn't want to lose it." Other than that he had just about given up.

> I didn't care about anything anymore. I'd spend weeks in the house, weeks in a motel, shooting dope from morning to night. I was keeping my stuff out in the open, not even bothering to hide it. I'd just get up, open the drawer, get off, go downstairs, eat, throw up, get off again . . . I'd rob a drug store, then lay up in a motel with a woman just for the company, to have someone to shoot dope with. I wasn't even interested in doing anything sexually. Then after a month or so I'd come out and hit another drug store to replenish my stash.
>
> By then I looked like a refugee from a concentration camp: hollow eyes, skin turning yellow, very little flesh on my bones, weighing maybe a hundred twenty pounds. I stayed away from mirrors because I knew I felt just the way I looked. Sometimes, though, I couldn't help but look in the mirror, and a mirror can be the world's greatest force for change.

"There are always glimpses of reality, in the mirror and elsewhere," says Don. "You may not do anything about them at the time, but you remember them." One glimpse came when Don went back to Lexington in the mid-sixties and recalled an incident that had occurred there years before.

> I was only nineteen when I first went to Lexington. We younger guys acted pretty cocky around the wards, and it made the old-timers angry. One of them pointed at me and said that he had once sat in the same chair I was sitting in. He was trying to give me a message, telling me that this thing wasn't a joke. I couldn't take it seriously, though,

> because I couldn't identify with a decrepit old guy like that. But I remembered him when I got back there six or seven years later. Here I was, sitting in that same chair, and the years in between had been devastating. I had lost a lot more, and I was getting tired.

In those last years Don spent a lot of time in treatment, sometimes to get out of a jail sentence and sometimes of his own volition, because by then he was really scared. In those years he saw the insides of several state hospitals in at least two states. He saw patients who had wine sores all over their bodies, patients who had broken their legs falling out of the empty buildings that winos sleep in. He saw doctors who didn't have licenses, doctors who couldn't speak English, doctors who barricaded themselves behind glass partitions because they feared violence from patients, doctors who couldn't see well enough to tell a patient from a coat rack. And he saw nurses who knew all about what an alcoholic hangover was, but whose attitude toward addict patients (as Don saw it) was "How could these awful people do those awful things with needles?" Don had to have all his wits about him to keep some perspective on these unsettling experiences.

> I knew that I would live to walk out of those places, but some people never would. When I was younger I overestimated my own control over situations. From kicking habits and beating jail terms I thought I could work my way into and out of things as I chose by sizing up situations, using my verbal skills, and being aggressive or tactful as needed. I learned there how little control people have over their fate.

At this time there was no methadone maintenance, no groups, no workshops. Addiction treatment consisted of Thorazine and individual psychiatric counseling. These treatments did not work for Don. As Jerry says, if you don't have a strong support group in treatment, the group support you get on the street will outweigh any new awareness you may be getting. And as Lee says, you can't give up addiction and all that it means (the "high," the identity, the group support) unless you have positive alternatives.

Don's last big stretch in treatment was a year in Norwich State Hospital. Facing the likelihood of a long sentence for robbing drug stores, he knew he couldn't beat the rap just by going in for a few weeks to detox. He had to bargain for a long enough commitment to demonstrate his "sincerity" in seeking rehabilitation. Since no one ever volunteered for a year in Norwich, his request made an impression on the authorities. He was sitll manipulating. He didn't expect much treatment, and, by his own account, he didn't get much.

> It was a wasted year. I spent it roaming around the dayroom like a caged but pacified animal. They kept me so doped up with Thorazine I could hardly move. And they'd wake me up at night to give me five or six grains of Nembutol to sleep with — me, a so-called drug addict. When they discharged me, it was with a year of that — a pill addiction habit!

Don believes that the patients were heavily drugged in order to keep the building quiet; he may be right. He speaks with understandable bitterness of the way our "chemophilic society" uses drugs in place of understanding and lets people like himself suffer wasted years and wasted lives for lack of proper teaching. Still, we cannot overlook the fact that Don over the years has bargained with many doctors to get the depressant drugs for which he expresses such disdain here. Speaking from a more recent perspective, he may not fully recall by whose initiative he received those medications in Norwich.

Restored to health (or the appearance thereof) by his year in the hospital, Don was given an eight-year suspended sentence. Back on the street, with no skills and no friends except in the drug crowd, he started using again. In a few months he was strung out, had hepatitis, and was ducking his probation officer. But his probation officer wasn't ducking him. "You've got eight years hanging," he warned. "I could send you back there right now, you know!"

Now, however, there was another option. Under a new drug treatment law scheduled to go into effect on October 30, 1967, Connecticut would be beginning a methadone maintenance program such as the one New York was already running. Don's probation officer wanted to get him into the program, and Don, facing the alternative of eight years in prison, agreed. In the meantime, he went back to Norwich, where he detoxed and spent four months in treatment for hepatitis. When he came out he had three weeks to wait for methadone. "All I needed was to get busted and sent up again with three weeks to go!" Yet Don does not seem to have considered the possibility of doing without drugs for three weeks. Instead, he went to an alcoholic doctor ("a guy who helps a lot of drunks, but can't help himself," according to Lee) who gave him Dilaudid, a morphine-derivative pill that is a little stronger than empirin or codeine and that dissolves in water to form an injectable solution. Thus fortified, he waited.

"That was the end of ten years of pursuing something so I wouldn't have to face myself," said Don in happier times. Whether it *was* the end remains to be seen.

***

At the end of 1964 Lee took a whole bottle of sleeping pills, then told his wife what he had done. She, of course, immediately took him to the hospital. Lee's allowing himself to be rescued expressed a degree of ambivalence in the death wish that he was to carry around for another five years. Many times during those years he felt that he wanted nothing more than to die. At least, he didn't want to go on living as he had been. Seeing no alternatives, he felt helpless, hopeless. It seemed that there was no way out.

While he was considering what he could do to put himself back together again, he got a call from a friend who invited him to come back to Connecticut and work in real estate. Florida had been his escape from Connecticut; now Connecticut was to be his escape from Florida — and (so he thought) from himself.

Lee had been hired to be his old self: hotshot salesman, bundle of energy, hail-fellow-well-met. Here he was, coming back to his old turf, billed as the hard-drinking, two-fisted Lee that everyone knew and loved so well. Only thing was, he wasn't drinking. One can imagine his boss's surprise when in walked a depressed, withdrawn guy. "What's the matter? Where's Lee?" said his boss. "What's the matter? Where's Lee?" said his parents, with whom he was living while he moved his wife and children back from Florida. Lee knew where "Lee" was and how to bring him back. Finally, after about two months, he did what any self-respecting drunk would do; he started drinking again. That brought back the old Lee. "I felt better, and everyone around me felt better," he recalls. Ironically, as soon as he started drinking again, everyone seemed to love him again. They didn't love and appreciate Lee; they loved and appreciated the caricature of Lee that he and they had created.

Now Lee was back in the congenial role of a traveling consultant — opening real estate projects, selling industrial land, doing advertising and promotion, and, of course, entertaining. Part of his job was to hustle women for clients in New York. There had been no courses at the Harvard Business School to prepare him for this side of the business world. He was a high class pimp — another thing he thought he would never stoop to. There were three-day weekends in New York, three-day blackouts in which he woke up in hotel rooms (sometimes all banged up, his clothes ruined) not knowing what he had done and who he had been with the night before. There were midnight bus rides and train rides from Hartford to New York and back. "Every form of seedy society and me, passing around our bottles and singing. Me, Harvard Business School graduate, business entrepreneur." There was a "night on the town" when he found himself in a tenement with his back against the wall and a knife against his throat.

> A hundred bucks poorer, I ran to the nearest police station demanding action. I was pounding the desk with indignation while the cops looked at

> me like I was crazy. They said I was lucky to have my head still on my shoulders. Finally they took me back in a cruiser to the Hotel Pierre — where I could have some more drinks on my account. Here drinking had almost gotten me killed, and the first thing I did was start in again.

During this period Lee ruined his father's retirement party with an evening-long binge that he explained away by saying that his feeling for his father had gotten the best of him. With silence and misguided "understanding" the people around Lee supported his denial system. Doris, his wife, tried to break through it, but she couldn't hold out by herself against his remorse and his conning, and their relationship degenerated into apathy. Life became a stale act, especially the morning after a blackout.

> You have to look knowing, act like you're on top of everything. You can't act like it was too funny, because it might not have been funny, but you can't act too sad, because it might have been funny. You have to walk a tightrope, noncommittal but alert for cues, until you can piece enough details together to satisfy yourself that you didn't kill anybody.

He didn't actually kill anybody even when he tried. Fed up with his whole act, he drove up an entrance ramp to Interstate 91 and deliberately crashed into the guard rail at the top. He intended to go through the rail and take a big drop to the roadway below, but he didn't hit it hard enough. The rail held, and he passed it off as an accident.

Eventually, with the help of a decent psychiatrist, he pulled himself out of his malaise. He began a year-long period of "controlled" drinking, in which he successfully cut down his intake and for the most part avoided the bad bouts. His life was sufficiently well balanced to support his exercise of will power, but the amount of will power required was prodigious. The preoccupation with drinking, the constant measuring of amounts, the ever-present thought that "this is dangerous for me" all testified to the compulsion that lay beneath the control. It seemed as if his alcoholism was in remission, but control was actually due to circumstance.

At this time Lee regained enough confidence in himself to leave his employer after two years and go into the industrial photographic equipment business. Drinking again took over his life under the cover of business entertainment. The local country club commemorated his exploits with a well-earned trophy. The inscription read, "Swingingest Swinger of Them All."

Lee characterizes his life from about 1966 on as "insane."

> I couldn't stop the fears from coming on, the fear of blackouts, fear of the unknown, fear of impeding disaster. I was getting too nervous to drive a car, and I couldn't sleep at night. I'd go home and pass out at seven or eight in the evening, wake up at ten, and be up the rest of the night. Or I'd come home drunk after lunch, pass out, and when I woke up at night I'd think it was the next morning. My kids thought that was so funny that one day they tricked me and pretended it was the next day, and I rushed around getting my shirt and tie as if I believed I was missing an important appointment.

It hurt to have to deceive others, but it hurt most of all to have to deceive himself.

> I'd buy my booze in a lot of different places, so that nobody (including myself) would add up how much I was buying. I'd charge my purchases at all the stores, have my secretary handle the bills, and then make a token cash purchase each month to prove to myself how little I was buying. I used to keep twelve bottles in the closet and drink a little from each in turn. Why? So I wouldn't be emptying any one bottle too quickly. That was the madness operating.

Lee's business failed when someone he had merged with turned out to have misrepresented his financial condition. Nobody caught it in time, "least of all myself, riddled with alcohol and greed, intent on the big windfall I should have known was too good to be true." So what did Lee do about it? He drank. "First I drank because I was making money, then I drank because I was losing money. After a while any excuse was good enough, till it got to the point where I was simply drinking between drinks."

During his last two years of drinking Lee blacked out regularly, and on fewer drinks. He was losing his tolerance for alcohol. In the final months he would check his pockets in the morning and find to his amazement that he still had most of the money he had started out with the night before. He couldn't believe how few drinks he had bought — and drunk — before blacking out.

That last year brought several rude jolts. After Lee had been dry for a few months he and Doris innocently agreed that he could have "one drink" at a family affair. Neither of them could have foreseen that that drink would last twelve hours or that Lee would "make the whole place a disaster area." In the painful confrontation with Doris that followed this fiasco, Lee brought out his last excuse, the one that "something in our manipulative systems tell us to hold back on, because we're going to need it when we've used up all the others." He told Doris, "I have a drinking problem. Please bear with me while I'm working on it."

It's one thing, however, when your wife complains about your drinking. It's quite another thing, as Lee says, "when the guys you crawl with say you're a pain in the ass." Even with Lee picking up the tab for most of the drinks, his "friends" began telling him that he was sloppy and obnoxious, that he was "trouble." That scared him. But his reaction was to find someone who could keep up with his drinking as his friends no longer could. He hooked up with a woman in Boston. As with Don and the women he shot up with in motels, sex was mostly beside the point by now. It was just the companionship of sharing the one thing that was left.

> Once I woke up with this woman in a hotel room. I caught a glimpse in the mirror of the whole scene — me all puffy, unshaven, hung over, sick, her spread out on the bed, not having had a bath for days, fat and sloppy like myself. I didn't see it then as a revelation that was going to make me stop, but just at that moment something got through to me of what an animal-like existence this was.
>
> One evening I was at her apartment in back of Fenway Park. It was raining cats and dogs — literally, as it turned out, because this monstrous little dog that the woman kept got out of the apartment and ran down the fire escape. The woman, who was drunk, started screaming for her only full-time companion, and I ran out into the rain and down four flights of stairs in my undershorts to hunt up that dog in the mud. And I just had to step back and look at that scene and what it told me about myself: Happiness is having a million-dollar business and rolling around in the mud in your undershorts looking for a little dog in the rain.

These were flashes of awareness, like the ones Don spoke of in his last years on heroin. They were telling Lee, "Hey, this is crazy. Something has to change." There were also positive flashes, like a South American winter vacation that Lee took with Doris (practically his first vacation ever), during which he did very little drinking. As the pain became greater, Lee was experiencing the three stages of growth that he talks about in *Consider the Alternative:* "I won't," "I can't," "Maybe I can." Like anyone approaching what for him or her represents the bottom, Lee was beginning to glimpse a way back up in the idea (and the feeling) that "Maybe I can."

This was how he understood these "flashes" in retrospect. But at the time the only alternative he saw was death. He read and reread John Donne's poems, wrote long, literary suicide notes, and pressed imaginary pistols to his temple. He played with death for quite some time, thinking that he wanted to die but just didn't have the guts to do away with himself. Even at that he was a failure. So he would have to pay somebody else to do it for him.

There followed an episode which stands out in Lee's career as the "trial by boiling water" stands out in Don's. Like Don, Lee had to choose between one form of self-destruction and another.

> In a bar that I used to frequent in another New England city I had been introduced to someone who, I was told, was connected with a crime syndicate. In my crazy world there was a lot of glamor in that, so I made friends with him. He turned out to be a decent guy. I visited him whenever I was in the area and did him favors (like lending him money). In the back of my mind I must have had the idea that I could use him someday.
>
> When the business started to go down and I got into financial trouble I let him in on what was happening and what my partner had done to me. He suggested that we burn the place. He would get a percentage of the insurance payoff, and he guaranteed that I would come out of it clean. But I was too nervous to take that chance, and I vetoed the idea.
>
> As things got even worse, both with the business and with my drinking, I got really depressed. So I went to him with another story. I told him that I had an incurable disease and had only a very short time to live. Using the kind of indirect request with which I had always manipulated doctors, I said, "If I could find somebody who could do it quickly so I wouldn't have to go through these last painful months, they'd be doing me a big favor. Besides, I have a lot of insurance that's going to be paid either way, and some it will pay double indemnity on an

accidental death."

In fact, the business had taken out $700,000 in life insurance on me the year before. That would wipe out the entire business debt, leaving the rest of my insurance for my family. But they wouldn't pay off on a suicide. "No problem," said my friend. His people could run me off the turnpike, and he would guarantee that it would look like an accident. All he wanted out of it was $5000, payable in advance.

I made the deal, then got cold feet. The idea of getting myself killed scared me enough to make me stop drinking, and without the immediate misery of the drinking I wasn't so desperate to die. So I postponed the execution of the "contract." I told the guy that I had some details to take care of first.

The postponement lasted while Lee stayed dry for several weeks. When he resumed drinking, it was for the last time.

I remember that last week of drinking. It scared me how tired and detached I had become. My attitude was: "Gee, look, I fell down a flight of stairs." "Gee, there's me, smashing up a car." "Gee, look at that business just going to pieces." A multi-million-dollar business was going down, the bank was calling in a four-hundred-thousand-dollar note, and I'd sit in a bar watching it happen as if it were some sports event they were showing on the TV.

I was letting go of everything. I stopped arguing with my wife. I didn't even bother with the manipulations any more, the remorse and the apologies. I was finished with everything. And probably that letting go was part of the final surrender that was coming. Even the business I had to let go of to do what I had to do for myself.

He was ready even to let go of his life. For he had given his syndicate friend the green light on the "contract." On what was to be his last day of drinking, Lee got up early and drove to the city where this man operated for a breakfast meeting at the top of a Holiday Inn. There he was to pay the $5000 and make the final arrangements. On the way he reviewed his twenty years of drinking. He had tried hospitals, psychiatrists, medication, moving, changing jobs, everything. There was nothing left to try. There was only death.

Lee looked down from the rooftop restaurant and thought of all the hotel windows from which he had wanted to jump. Meanwhile, the man with whom he had made the "contract" never showed up. Lee stood there, shabby, unshaven, shaking with a hangover from the night before. He knew now that, if he wanted to go on living, he would have to live without alcohol, his constant companion and "answer" to every problem and every need. He surrendered to the fact that he couldn't control it, couldn't beat it. He had to give it up — but what would that mean?

From the Holiday Inn he called a doctor friend and arranged to be put in the hospital for a five-day, self-supervised detox. Then he drove home. Thus, at eleven A.M. on October 15, 1969, Lee cried and took his last few sips of vodka as he left the house to take a cab to the hospital.

> Even then I gave a story to the cab driver (a drinking buddy) to explain why I was going to the hospital: "I'm going in for tests, Joe. Don't tell those friends of ours down at the bar, but I think I have an ulcer." Con man to the end. Half of me was feeling that I was ending one way of life, while the other half was saying that it was too much a part of me to give up.
>
> I often wonder what would have happened that morning if the guy I was supposed to meet had shown up, or if I hadn't reached my friend the doctor, or if I had jumped from the fourteenth floor. Really, I don't know.

Lee had lived with an intense vision of death, but when it came to a choice, he did not choose death. It was not that he wanted to die, but that he didn't want to go on living as he had been living. Later he cancelled the "contract" by saying that his doctors had discovered that his "terminal illness" had been a diagnostic error. Yet underneath the cover story (as with other such stories that he, Don, and Jerry told) there was a foundation of truth. Lee had what he thought was the hopeless, incurable disease of alcoholism (which was, in fact, about to kill him). Then, by a miracle, he was cured.

> It was fate, or faith, whatever. October 15, 1969, was the last day of twenty years of making bargains with God to help me control what could not be controlled. It all happened because somewhere along the line I had learned that I should be able to succeed without failure, to love without loss, to reach out without risk of disappointment, to have pleasure without pain. It happened because long ago I had learned that I could not risk letting myself feel.

***

Nothing ever changes in the world of addiction. People who choose addiction are looking for a safe, sure, predictable sensation. Their whole lives are set up to guarantee sameness. Year after year, as in Saroyan's *The Time of Your Life,* the same people sit on the same stools in the same bars. When a friend of Lee's in Alcoholics Anonymous went into a bar to pick up someone who had passed out there, the bartender said to him, "You son of a bitch. I told you to stay out of here, and here you are back." It had been five years since that man had been in that bar.

So when Jerry went back to his old haunts to "see what the fellas are doing," he knew very well what the fellas were doing. They had been doing the same thing from time immemorial and probably are doing the same thing today. Jerry bumped into a friend whose greeting after a three-year absence was, "I got $3.25. You got $3.75?" That meant that they could get four two-dollar bags for seven dollars. Jerry, knowing that he had no tolerance after three years of clean living, took only one of the four bags for himself. Even the one sent him out for a while. It was his one near-fatal overdose.

In a matter of months, although he was not strung out and was still productive as a shoe salesman, Jerry's drug use was sufficiently visible that his parole officer told him he'd better get out of New York. He applied for a job managing the shoe department in E.J. Korvett's in Hartford, which A.S. Beck had just contracted to run. He got the job, and with it a new parole officer and a new lease on life.

In Hartford Jerry lived a double life, working during the week and making runs to New York for dope on weekends. But there were times when he didn't go back quite so often, times when he didn't go back at all. For now he was socializing with new people who didn't know his past and accepted him at face value. He began to go out with a cashier in the children's department named Joanne. Here was a woman who cared about him who wasn't a junkie herself.

After about a year of relative happiness, Jerry was busted for possession in the summer of 1963. "Down the tubes again," he figured stoically. But something strange happened. Joanne, whose traditional Italian background had not prepared her for Jerry's strange ways, showed unexpected resourcefulness by telling the parole officer that she wanted to marry Jerry and help him start a new life. And A.S. Beck, instead of firing him, transferred him to a new store on Fifth Avenue in New York. It was a real break for Jerry.

Jerry was now poised between his old life and and a new one that beckoned to him. He was at a moment of choice. The ambivalence he felt about it is shown by the fact that when he moved back to New York with Joanne, they took an apartment in the Grand Concourse of the Bronx, six or seven blocks from his old neighborhood. They could have lived in any of the other boroughs of New York, but Jerry (though he was trying to be clean at the time) chose to live in a place where he could not help being drawn back into the drug scene. Such was the tenacity of his old identity.

Two representatives of the straight society, Joanne and A.S. Beck, had shown some faith in Jerry. It was a start, but it wasn't enough to overcome twenty-eight years of narrow experience and self-defeating thinking. Despite his proven proficiency in deviant activities, despite his initial success as a salesman and store manager, Jerry still did not credit himself with the aptitude to succeed in the straight world. Not having accomplished much, he saw no reason to believe that he could accomplish much. He "didn't have much in the bank — emotionally, psychologically, financially — and the drugs were a perfect shield from that." Moreover, he thought it was his lot in life to steal from his employer, to cheat on his wife, and to exploit both of them in order to stay out of jail. If they only knew him, he thought, if they only knew what he was and what values he lived by, they wouldn't want to have anything to do with him. Because they didn't know, he got some support from them, but he couldn't be honest with them. There was no one with whom he could honestly share his doubts and dilemmas — not Joanne, not A.S. Beck, not his parole officer.

After several drug-free months Jerry got bored with rent payments and car payments. He got bored with walking around a tiny efficiency apartment and bumping into a wife who had no friends in the area. He took a longer walk — back to his old turf and to his double life. Not only was he using drugs, but he was beginning to steal from the shoe store.

Late in 1964, with one son born and another on the way, he was busted again. He lost his job and with it his ability to provide for his children. Joanne had had enough; she left him and went back to live with her parents in Hartford. As he continued to catch cases for minor offenses (possession and works), Jerry felt very alone. "The only involvement I had was with my old group of friends, the same old faces. They'll always take you back."

After a year spent fighting cases and serving a short prison term, Jerry went back to his Italian contacts. His credit was good with them. "I had gone to jail, kept my mouth shut; I was what's known as a thoroughbred. So I was back in business, bigger than ever before."

The year 1966 was a rerun of 1958. It was a dark period of relentless activity, pressure, and suspicion. Keeping things together on the street was tougher than ever. Ten years earlier it was a cinch to cash a stolen check. Now the trust that Jerry, Don, and many others had abused was no longer there to be abused. When Jerry tried to pass off a bogus check in a check cashing place in the Bronx, he found himself locked inside the store while the man behind the caged desk was calling the police. He had to throw a chair through the window to get out.

After another incredible ten-month run of dealing without a bust, Jerry caught three cases in a row, two of them sales. His bail was set so high that he couldn't make it. In January, 1967, he said goodbye to the light of day and descended into the notorious New York detention center known as the Tombs. He was facing big time.

His public defender told him that the state would give him ten to twenty years if he copped a plea. That was unreasonable, replied Jerry. He was holding out for seven and a half to fifteen. For that difference he stayed in the Tombs, fighting and delaying, for a year and a half — time to which he had never been sentenced. Since it counted toward fulfillment of his eventual sentence, however, he figured he had nothing to lose.

But it was grueling time. This was Jerry's first stretch of any duration in an adult prison. The relatively benign character of Elmira and Chillicothe, and of their inmates (in the 1950s), stemmed from the fact that both of these institutions were reformatories for youthful offenders. One could have a prolonged adolescence there and enjoy it. The Tombs showed Jerry what it meant to be grown up and still be on the wrong side of the fence.

> The place was designed for you to do thirty days and go to trial, not for a long stretcn. The building was connected directly to the court building at 60 Centre Street, so you never saw daylight, even when you went to court. And since everybody who came in was transient, I never had a chance to build up a community there as I had in other institutions. I must have seen a couple of hundred cellmates come and go.

By his own testimony, Jerry did not undergo a change of awareness or attitude in the Tombs. His reaction to the treatment centers that were then opening up, like Daytop Village, was to call the participants "faggots." All his efforts went toward getting out, just as they had at Elmira sixteen years before. He was still scrambling for survival.

> I fought cases, changed pleas, tried to bargain, asked for changes of venue, fired one public defender and got another. I wrote to rabbis, lawyers, anyone who might help me get a break. I portrayed myself as a small fry dealer, a junkie myself, not hurting anybody, just wanting to have my habit and be left alone. I pleaded circumstances, saying I never had a break, and all I wanted was one break. I fought as long as I could, figuring that maybe they would get tired.

But it was he who was getting tired. It was he who felt himself aging. He was clean, healthy, and in possession of all his faculties. His was the desperation of a strong man who was reaching the limit of his endurance.

When he went before the court for his plea and trial date, he got a break. He had no idea how big a break it would be. A Russian Jewish judge who had had it in for him had retired. Instead, he came before a black judge, Judge Gregory. It is a story that he still delights in telling to his counseling students:

> I stood before the court with my counsel while the D.A. shuffled through some papers at his table. "Young man," said the judge, "have you ever been away for treatment?" I had had one brief stay in Lexington, but I wasn't going to tell him that. "No, Your Honor," I said. I was beginning to hear mumblings from the D.A.'s table, but I didn't want to turn around. I heard the judge ask, "What would you do if the court recommended you for treatment for your addiction?" At this the D.A. practically exploded off the table. "Your Honor," he sputtered, "this

> defendant is one of the biggest and most notorious dealers in the East Bronx. His record does not indicate that he is a candidate for rehabilitation. The people of the state of New York recommend . . ." The judge told him that the court would decide. Then he said to me. "You know, I'm going to take a big chance on you. If you were eighteen now, chances are that you would go into a treatment program. But they didn't have such programs back when you got started with drugs. Would you accept a criminal commitment?" I said, "Yes, Your Honor, I certainly would." And the D.A. just kept mumbling in the back.
>
> It was unreal. Not in my wildest dreams did I anticipate a break like that. To me, if I had asked the D.A. for that, I would have been the one who was unreasonable.

It was 1968. In 1967, while Jerry was finagling in the Tombs, the Rockefeller Act had been passed, enabling addicts to get treatment.

6
surrender

"It's amazing," says Lee. "Twenty years of drinking and pill-taking, just to feel as good as I do now without any chemical substitutes. It's been a whole new life these past ten years. I get my highs from life now — from being with my family, from helping people, from seeing a sunrise."

How did it happen? How did Lee, Don (for a time), and Jerry make what is called the "recovery turn"? How can others do the same? Lee teaches that recovery has two essential ingredients. The first is a supportive atmosphere that offers unconditional love, trust, warmth, nourishment, and safety. The second consists of alternatives to self-destructive behavior. A person isn't going to give up something that "feels good" without having other choices, other options.

For many people, recovery begins with what the late Harry M. Tiebout, a psychiatrist, called an "act of surrender." Surrender is a deep, largely unconscious movement. In response to changes in one's environment, one experiences a "moment of readiness" in which one no longer needs to fight, to deny and defy reality.

According to Tiebout,

> When that happens, the individual is wide open to reality; he can listen without conflict and fighting back. He is receptive to life, not antagonistic. He senses a feeling of relatedness and at-oneness which becomes the source of an inner peace and serenity . . . [1]

This act of surrender is followed (temporarily or permanently) by a state of surrender, in which one continues to accept reality and live in harmony with it.

Tiebout illustrates the concept of surrender by telling the story of an alcoholic. An alcoholic's defiance and grandiosity are so pronounced as to make it easy to observe when he "lets go." Nonetheless, Lee has used the concept of surrender successfully in working with people who cling to any kind of destructive behavior. "Whatever habit you're locked into," he says, "whatever form of death you've gone through, the experience of becoming emotionally free of it is the same." In this chapter Lee's surrender as an alcoholic leads into Don's and Jerry's somewhat different experiences of surrender. If these accounts at moments sound overblown it is because surrender indeed is a moment of heightened engagement with life.

***

Webster defines "miracle" as "an unexplained happening." That is how Lee remembers his surrender.

> There was no apparent reason for it to happen on that day rather than any other. It was the one and only time I gave up drinking without self-pity. I no longer resented giving up that life, no longer felt deprived. It wasn't like I was abstaining and gritting my teeth. I didn't miss it. I could have seen it all around, I could have been bathing in it, and I wouldn't have missed it.

In fact, one reason Lee wouldn't think of taking a drink now is that he has no assurance that he could ever get sober again. "How do I know that I could go through the same thing I went through in '69? I never could before; maybe I never could again."

Although Lee, following a tradition of Alcoholics Anonymous, celebrates the anniversary date of his sobriety, even for him that date took on meaning only in retrospect. As he says,

> If I watch the sun come up in the morning, there is no way I can tell exactly when the sun is up and when it isn't. There's no one demarcation point, just a hazy area when it crosses over, when you can't tell the difference between night time and dawn. That's what recovery is like.

At the time Lee sensed only that "something felt different this time." When he went to the hospital he left a note for Doris saying that she could visit him or not, leave him or not, as she chose. The letter wasn't a "con job"; it was sincere. "I told her that this time, if I was going to do something, I was going to do it for me. I didn't even know what 'it' was, but I knew that I was sick of being sick."

Doris did come to visit him with the children, and she did not leave him. His sister also came and got him to promise to go to an A.A. meeting. Years before, when Lee knew all the answers, he had thrown away the first A.A. literature he ever saw. "To me A.A. was hellfire and tambourines, sour faces and religious songs." Now, though, he promised to go to one meeting because "I really didn't want to go back to booze. I really wanted to do something." Part of his surrender was the admission that he didn't know all the answers.

In a sense, surrender is something that happens in a day. In another sense, it takes the rest of one's life. Surrender is a process, not an event. It has to be reinforced if it is to endure. For Lee the reinforcement came first at A.A.

Lee's first meeting was on a cold October night.

> I hung around outside shivering for a half an hour until a guy noticed me and asked me if I was

> looking for A.A. "Yes," I mumbled, and he said, "Step inside." I did, and a year later he told me that he should have gone in with me because that night he slipped and got drunk. One comes in, one goes out.

At these early A.A. meetings (which he attended at least once a day) Lee learned lessons that others can learn even if their addiction is not to alcohol and their support group is not A.A. The most important lesson was printed on a sign that Lee saw on the wall the first time he walked into an A.A. meeting: "You Are Not Alone Anymore." When a former police detective who had lost everything in life to alcoholism spoke of his fear of being alone and the insanity of his life, Lee thought, "Gee, our backgrounds are different, but I've had those feelings, too." That was what another A.A. saying, "Don't compare; identify," meant to Lee. Here were ordinary, familiar, recognizable people, not Skid Row derelicts, who had been through the same things Lee had. "We're so wrapped up in our own insanity that we don't realize how many people out there are just like us."

The other big surprise was that these people were laughing. From their laughter Lee picked up a message of hope: "These people were doing it, so maybe I could, too." When he got home he told his wife, "I don't know, Doris, but I think I've found something, because I felt different when I came out of there." He felt comfortable. He felt "the way I had felt when I was sitting at a bar — that I belonged, that I had come home, that these people were my people."

A.A. taught Lee that he was powerless over alcohol; there was no way he could drink safely (Step 1). But he could accept that lesson because A.A. simultaneously gave him a source of strength and support that was better than alcohol — people.

> Father John Powell[2] says that it only takes a moment to be loved a whole life through. What A.A. gave me was love — people caring and not judging me or putting me down. If love is to be effective, it has to be unconditional. There can't

> be any fine print in the expression of love. I had always heard people tell me, "I'll love you if . . .," "I'll love you until . . ." "I'll love you except . . .," "I'll love you but . . ." A.A. gave me unconditional love.
>
> At the same time they challenged me. They didn't let me get away with anything. And I needed that, too. I was still "conning," still hedging, when I made sure to tell Doris that they talked a lot about "slips" at A.A. That was a little insurance that the old insurance salesman took out.

Knowing that it's a lot easier to stop choosing addiction than to stay stopped, Lee worked to learn the concepts of A.A., like the Serenity Prayer and the "one day at a time" concept. He learned to distinguish between his wants and needs, thereby gaining a new perspective on the collapse of his business. When he had to travel on business, he found out that there were A.A. groups all over the map where he could feel at home. If there was any situation that evoked his past life, it was a business trip. But as a friend in A.A. reminded him, "Lee, the sobriety in Phoenix is just like the sobriety in Hartford." Wherever he traveled Lee was still himself, just as when he tried and failed to put geographical distance between himself and his drinking. Only now it was his new, sober self that he carried with him.

Lee was learning to cope with difficult things without drinking, and he was learning fast.

> It wasn't easy; I still had a lot of bad habits to cure. Drinking is made up of thinking, "stinking thinking." To clean up my drinking I had to clean up my mind, my attitudes. I never really had any trouble with drinking. I had trouble with living and thinking.

In this respect Lee was no different from a person who smokes or overeats. The problem isn't with cigarettes or food; the problem is with living and thinking. In prodding Lee to reexamine his "stinking thinking," the people in A.A. were giving him the same insight that he was later to find in the work of Albert Ellis. He drew upon their support and followed all the steps they laid out. "I think that if they had told me to go jump off a bridge, I would have done it."

As this last remark suggests, Lee's initial involvement with A.A. was a total involvement. It was not, however, a passive one. Lee was able to grow within that involvement by working at his recovery — listening closely, putting together his own thoughts, sharing experiences in the discussion groups, exchanging phone numbers with his fellow members.

> I started expressing myself and having some confidence in myself. "You know, he's not all bad," I'd say about myself. And the humiliation and degradation slowly began to lift. I was finding a joy and fulfillment that I had never had before. For the first time I was feeling happy and comfortable without chemicals, and I felt my life changing. In the discussion groups I started being honest about myself. I like being honest. The next thing I knew, I was being honest outside of the A.A. meetings. People starting looking at me differently; they didn't know what was happening to me.

As part of learning to "identify" rather than "compare," Lee finally broke down and went to a meeting at the Salvation Army, which he had been avoiding because he thought he would surely find tambourines and brimstone there. Once he went to one Salvation Army meeting, he never missed one for months. There a magnetic Irishman named Danny taught him the "first-drink" concept.

> I used to get up in the morning and wonder which drink had got me the night before — the sixth? the tenth? No it was the first. If I hadn't had the first drink I wouldn't have got drunk. Amazing! How many thousands of times had I contemplated which drink did it to me? If I hadn't taken the first one I never would have had to worry about it.

There, too, he saw the people who really had it bad. Lee had problems, but nothing like the ones he heard at the Salvation Army. "I at least had a home, a family, three square meals, money jingling in my pocket. Yet those people's feelings, their wounds were just like mine."

Lee did have money jingling in his pocket, and that made it easier for him to concentrate on his recovery. With a million-dollar business, even one that was going under, there was so much money coming in that Lee had no problem drawing out what he needed to support his family. After the business was liquidated he could still count on his wife's income plus additional financial support from his family. So he could afford a pause in his working life.

Still, there was pain — pain that in the past would have provided ample excuses for drinking.

> My life during my first months of sobriety was no bed of roses. My business was headed for bankruptcy. I discovered that one of my dearest friends and employees was stealing from me, and I had to confront him about it. I sued someone for a substantial sum, only to have the court decide that I owed him money. For some unspecified reason I was blackballed from an organization

> which it had been my lifelong ambition to join and whose meetings I had been attending after I was already sober. All of these things upset me, but I was able to accept them.
>
> Then I had to watch my mother die of cancer. She and my father had been away in Asia for four months. My goodbye to her had been a big blowup between me and my father when we were both drunk. Her illness became apparent right after they got home. I went through incredible guilt feelings: "Oh, if I had been a better son . . ." We didn't talk much when I visited her — in that respect it was the same way the family had always been — but she liked my coming to see her, and I found out later from my sister that she was quite pleased that I wasn't drinking. My father, too (who was himself to die suddenly two years later), gave me all kinds of explicit and implicit compliments on the way I was handling my life after I became sober — and that was a big change from our past relationship, although I came to accept that the change would never be complete.

During this period Lee went on living by the principles of A.A. and getting support from his new friends there, who gave him "not so much sympathy as understanding. They talked with me when I wanted to talk."

> All my life I was alone until I found booze; once I found booze I was alone until I found A.A. The day I found booze I found relief from pain. The day I found A.A. I found relief from booze.

***

Sometimes people do the right thing for the wrong reasons. Just as a troubled person may "back into" the negative solution of addiction (because the alternatives are even less palatable), so an addicted person may back into the positive solution of recovery. Recovery often begins when giving up the addiction has become the least unpalatable of the available options. Lee, Don, and Jerry all speak of a sense of "impending doom" as having pushed them toward recovery. That doom wasn't just a mystical vision; it was very concrete. It was death or long-term imprisonment. At the beginning of recovery all three men were in some sense choosing the lesser of two evils, as Don had years earlier when he chose a few seconds in scalding water over five years in jail. Such a choice, may, at the outset, provide the best motivation for cleaning up.

This was clearly the case with Don. Looking back at his decision to go into the methadone program at Blue Hills Hospital in Hartford, Don sees in it a kind of surrender.

> In retrospect I don't think I ever fully accepted the idea that I existed only to shoot dope, even though it looked that way. For ten years I had acted as if my life was meaningless and I didn't care what happened to me. But when it came down to going to prison for years, I must have decided that I really wanted my life. Even though I was acting expediently when I wiggled out of that sentence, even though I didn't know yet what methadone would do for me, I must have been making some fundamental positive decision when I wouldn't let them put me in prison.

At the time, however, he was most certainly "acting expediently." If Lee was still doing a little "conning" even after he had actually given up drinking (because he was not completely sure he had given it up), Don was engaged in outright manipulation when he went into the methadone program. Moreover, he had not given up illegal drug use.

When Don began on methadone he was still getting Dilaudid from a doctor. Within two days he stopped going to the clinic for the methadone because "the Dilaudid was better, a lot better." It wasn't long before he was brought back to the clinic by threats from the authorities. "I had to honor the program, go through the motions, even while I was getting my real high somewhere else." Still, it was a step. By being forced to participate in the program, Don could learn what the program was about — once the people who were running it figured out what it was about.

At this stage, Don's actions were governed by two considerations. On the one hand, he wanted the "high." On the other hand, he "had eight years hanging." In fairness to Don, though, he still was not being given alternatives other than the methadone itself. He also was not being given understanding and emotional support. As the first patient in the newly authorized Blue Hills methadone program — its *only* patient for several months — Don did not have workshop groups where he could share experiences and feelings as Lee did in A.A. The concept of the program was new to the staff as well. The doctors in charge had to overcome prejudices about drug users and about methadone maintenance. "What are we running here," they would say, "a British program? Are we supplying people?" Don would bring in articles about the methadone maintenance program already underway in New York and have shouting matches with the doctors about what constituted a maintenance dose.

Nor was there any counseling to speak of; that, too, was to be a field for Don's pioneering efforts in the months and years to come. A few of the nurses and social workers talked to Don from time to time, but mostly he was left to interpret his experience on his own (which meant that at the outset he would interpret it in his old ways). As yet they hadn't even thought of testing his urine to see if he was still shooting dope. In this primitive stage of addiction treatment, they just handed out pills. So Don would pick up his pills in the morning and spend the rest of the day taking care of business, reasserting his old routine, doing the only thing he knew how to do. He would go down to the corner and get high.

Don felt himself leading a double life, and not just in the sense that he was taking methadone and heroin at the same time.

> As before I was staying with my mother on and off, wherever I could find a place to stay. I was

> coming into contact with different kinds of people, and I was still walking around paranoid. I moved cautiously. I walked around alone, asking myself questions: Who did I know? Who could I trust? What was I going to do with my life? When I visited people I'd grown up with who didn't use drugs, I found we had little in common. Their regulated lives frightened me, and I felt out of place among their wives and children. A guy would talk about hunting, and I'd think about how the only hunting I'd done was in concrete cities. We could talk, but I was uneasy, I felt that they wondered what had happened to the person they used to have good times with. They didn't know who I had become. And yet that was my identity, and my life was still very much tied up in it. I didn't want to give it up, because it was all I had.

Again, it was a question of alternatives.

While Don was "in limbo, suspended between the mainstream of society and the cockroach-infested apartments I had known," he had an experience which pushed him decisively in one direction.

> The break came for me one day when they stopped a bunch of us and shook us down. All of a sudden it occurred to me that I wasn't sick, that the methadone by itself was holding me. That was my moment of awareness, when I said to myself, "What am I doing taking these kinds of risks with the police when I'm not sick?" I didn't need to take those risks for the drug anymore. And I think it was only then, when I began to feel some security from another source, that I could bear to open up and ask myself other questions like: "How many more times do I want to give up my rings to the cop man?" "How long can I go on knowing that in a few days the cop man will have

> the leather jacket I'm wearing now?" "How long can I keep giving somebody a piece of my flesh?" And I got to thinking about other things I could be doing instead.

If the authorities had just said to Don, "We'll give you a drug that will take away the pain just as heroin does, and you won't have to hustle all day and risk arrest to get it," he would have nodded and walked away. Even if he had understood and believed the words, he wouldn't have felt their implications. He needed to be shown. By having to come and get his pills even while he didn't yet believe in the program, he was able to experience directly what methadone could mean for him. He could begin to take part in the program for positive instead of negative reasons.

> Even in the first few months on methadone I knew my life was better. I felt cleaner, if only because I could bathe regularly. I was my own person now. For the first time I wasn't frightened, wasn't running scared from the moment I got up in the morning. Methadone did what heroin used to do for me — organized me, took out the cobwebs, let me get going. So I made a decision that I was going to make this work. I would take it one day at a time and see what came out of it.

That this choice was a real and very significant one is shown by what happened next. Don stopped using heroin; in his words, he "cut it loose." To make his decision stick he had to resist powerful gravitational forces pulling him back to his old ways.

> A week after the shakedown a friend who was just out of prison came over and took me for a ride to get some coffee. I noticed that he was high. At that moment I think I really grew. I thought about myself and realized that if I stayed with him, there would be another time and then another, and

eventually I would be using drugs myself again. So I told him that I was on methadone now and wanted nothing more to do with heroin. I told him that he would have to take me home or drop me off. He ranted and raved: Was I going crazy? Was I a cop? I got out at a traffic light and walked back home feeling good about myself.

When I got home I sat down and thought about what staying away from drugs was going to mean. I realized that my discipline would have to be absolute, not flexible. I understood then that I could not associate with anybody who was using drugs or be involved in any criminal activity. And it scared me, because the next week I might be back banging at their door, saying, "I'm sorry, I don't know what got into me. You understood. Can I get a bag of dope from you?" But I couldn't go back, even for conversation, because you just can't go back halfway. If you go back out of loneliness and a desire for companionship, you will have to take on the whole thing, and that means the bag of heroin.

Don understood that he could no more go back to his old friends "for conversation" than Jerry could go back to his pals in the Bronx without getting high or Lee could associate regularly with his ex-drinking buddies and not drink with them. These were not supportive groups that cared about a person unconditionally. Drug use was the badge of membership, and anyone who gave up that group's drug of choice would become straight, a square, a "faggot." Once he gave up heroin Don would be rejected just as he had rejected others who had given it up. His decision to give it up meant, therefore, that he would have to learn to call a different group of people "friends." Eventually he was to find new friends such as Lee and Jerry. For the time being, though, he was committing himself to a rather solitary life.

Left with what would otherwise be uneasy feelings about himself, he was not about to give up methadone.

> A couple of months after I started on the methadone, when I had already stopped using other drugs, a psychiatrist told me he couldn't understand why I came in for that medication every day. I said, "Well, then, you don't understand what I went through for ten years if you can't see why I take an hour out of each day to be a free man for the rest of the day." Methadone gave me time to work through the feelings I still wouldn't have been able to live with. It gave me time to find an identity for myself, to build a foundation for my life. I couldn't cut it loose because I was still too far down to look directly up to the top without some support.

Fair enough. The question is whether he ever did work through his feelings, find an identity, and build a foundation for his life. If he had, his giving up heroin for methadone would have been a major step in a successful recovery. From the perspective of his later career, however, it appears in a different light.

On the day of the police shakedown, when Don realized that methadone had freed him from his dependency on heroin, he had a surrender experience that was genuine, but limited. He was tired of paying the cop man and running afoul of the cops, but he did not question his need for a pain-relieving drug. On that day he surrendered the illegal drug heroin; he did not surrender the narcotic experience. He surrendered the cop man; he did not surrender the "high." What he gave up for good was the hard work, the risks, and the hardships of the street life, not the drug. That was his surrender.

***

When Jerry was given a five-year criminal commitment to a treatment center in Woodbourne, New York, he had one concern, and it was the same as Don's: to get out. Five years was a lot less time than the ten or twenty that Jerry had expected, but the name of the game was to get out, and Jerry was still playing the game.

He was not thinking in terms of rehabilitation.

Woodbourne was a converted prison; the state had changed the sign on the door from "Corrections" to "Mental Health." Jerry, who already knew most of his fellow inmates, was "back home and having fun." It was just like old times, except for the fact that inmates now had the option in participating in a treatment program, which consisted of meetings and workshop groups. Jerry chose not to do the program; that was for "faggots."

Then Jerry noticed something strange happening. People who had come to Woodbourne after him and who were taking part in the rehabilitation program were getting out before him. They were beating him at his own game. Jerry, who had trained himself to be alert to changing conditions on the street, quickly perceived that the state had changed the rules of the game on him. He would have to learn a new game.

The way out was education. When a black inmate "one-upped" Jerry in the dayroom by using big words that Jerry didn't understand, Jerry sat for thirty days in the library reading *Thirty Days to a Better Vocabulary.* He came out using words like "verisimilitude" and "maudlin." It was a small incident, but it showed Jerry that he could do something about his anger instead of just saying, "Man, am I dumb!"

He did the same thing when he took a correspondence course, Western Civilization 110, from Sullivan County Community College. "I wanted to see if I could pass a college course," he explains. "I thought I'd see what it was all about." This openness to experience was to be crucial to Jerry's recovery. All his life he had believed that he didn't have the skills to make it in straight society. Yet when he was given an incentive to test that assumption, he had the curiosity and the courage to do so. Having seen that the skills he had always relied on would get him a lifetime in jail, he had reached a "moment of readiness" to try out new directions. And the results were encouraging. "I did the readings, it was fun, and I got an A."

He also began to attend the group therapy sessions. He picked up expressions like, "I can relate to that," "Where are you coming from?" "I can identify with that," and "That's off the wall" as he once had picked up drug slang and prison slang. Some of the language was even the same, like "That's a copout," but the meaning was different here.

> Once I got involved, I couldn't help noticing that the guys who were running the program and doing the groups not only were getting out faster than I was, but also seemed to have a certain confidence about themselves and what they were doing. They were sure that they were going to the top because they had found a new magic to replace the magic of drugs. It had to make me reflect a little. Maybe I could do what they could do.

Readers of *Consider the Alternative* will recognize in Jerry's last sentence the expression "Maybe I can." Jerry had been defiant ("I won't"); he had felt fated or doomed ("I can't"); and now he was ready to listen and learn — and to change ("Maybe I can").

With Woodbourne filled to capacity, Jerry's progress in the groups plus his college credits got him out in eighteen months (instead of five years.) That was a reward right there. Meanwhile, counting his previous eighteen months in The Tombs, Jerry had been out of circulation for three years. He was almost thirty-five years old. "I can't go through this again," he thought. He was getting tired. For the first time his thinking was directed not only towards getting out, but *staying* out as well.

Jerry still wanted the good feelings. Like Don, he wanted the "high," but not the hassle. The difference was that Jerry was learning that there was another way of getting high, a way that did not involve drugs. He had an alternative.

> Now that I was learning new skills and the new therapeutic language, I no longer felt fated. I was no longer programmed to go down the same slide. While I was in Woodbourne I had heard somebody from Connecticut talking about the program at Blue Hills. Even back when I was

> living in Hartford I had heard vague references to Blue Hills. But now I heard two names mentioned — Jack Cohen, the head counselor, and Donald Pet, the chief psychiatrist. I came out with that information, plus the certainty that if I stayed in New York I would go back to the only neighborhood I knew there. And that was not what I wanted.

Jerry got out of Woodbourne in February, 1970. It was a Friday. He went to New York and got high for the weekend. Monday morning he was due to report to his aftercare worker for urinalysis and group work. He never showed up. By then he had left the state for good. Sunday night he had taken a train to Hartford, where he visited his two young sons. Monday morning he put on a suit and went to the Blue Hills Hospital drug rehabilitation clinic, where he presented himself as a veteran of the group work at Woodbourne, drug-free for three years.

> I went first to Jack Cohen and told him that Dr. Pet had sent me over for a job. If Donald Pet had been in that room with him, I wouldn't have known it. But Jack bought the story and allowed me to sit in groups that day. At the end of the day I went across the street and looked up Donald Pet. "Dr. Pet," I said, "I'm Jerry Edelwich. Jack Cohen sent me over for a job." He said he'd consider it, and I began attending groups every day. Of course, Jack Cohen and Donald Pet got together and discovered the trick I'd played on them. But instead of kicking me out, they said, "Fine. He's done this much; let's see what else he can do."

The con man was up to his old tricks, but for a new purpose.

That last heroin "high" that Jerry didn't mention to his new employers at Blue Hills was in fact the last he ever had. At the time, though, Jerry could not be sure that it would be his last, just as Lee could not be sure that he had taken his last drink the previous autumn. The fact that he did get high after coming out of Woodbourne indicates that even then he had not fully surrendered his drug use. By his own testimony, he was not safely beyond the temptation to use drugs for perhaps another two years.

7
rebirth

Recovery means leaving behind the inner loneliness and false sociability of addiction and reaching a state of being at peace with oneself and others. It begins when a person willingly accepts withdrawal along with whatever pain it entails. Recovery means building the foundation of a new life, a life that is more than the mere negation of an addictive dependency. If and when the foundation of such a life is set reasonably well in place, the person is no longer subject to the cycle of addiction and withdrawal described in *Love and Addiction.* It is then no longer meaningful to think of the person's psychic experience in those terms. Although the memory of past unhappiness and of the compensatory "high" is there, there is no longer an impulse to invoke that memory by acting it out. By that point, a new set of satisfactions has replaced the "high." Addiction is not an alternative.

It doesn't always happen that way, of course. Recovery is rarely uncomplicated and not always successful. Not everyone succeeds in building a strong enough foundation for a new life, at least on the first try. Anyone *can* do it; not everyone does. But for those who do make it, it is one of the most exciting passages that life can offer. It is like going from night to day, from sickness to health. No wonder recovering addicts speak of themselves as "reborn."

***

The principles which guided Lee's, Don's, and Jerry's recoveries are the same principles that they have since shared with others in their work as counselors and teachers. They are the principles by which Lee and Jerry have continued to live to this day. Lee, who has summarized these principles so effectively in *Consider the Alternative,* emphasizes that a helping relationship is an involvement between one person and another at a human, caring level.

> Involvement, as I first learned in A.A., is the creation of a loving atmosphere that lets people be comfortable enough with themselves to be able to change. Healing doesn't come from keeping an "objective" distance. It doesn't come from mystifying each other with labels, diagnoses, and interpretations. It doesn't come from raking up past history, from treating each other as if we were "sick," or from criticizing each other when we already lack self-confidence and a sense of wholeness. Healing comes from sensitivity and empathy and sharing. In my experience, we help not by substituting drugs and shock treatments for human relationships, but by caring, nourishing, and accepting. Thus I try to help people as I was helped in A.A., and as Don and Jerry and I in the early days at Blue Hills supported each other as well as our clients. I try to help people accept responsibility for their lives, clarify their values, and commit themselves to action. That is what I mean by facilitating change.

As Lee makes clear, this is not a non-directive, psychoanalytic therapy. Rather, it is based on three involvement-oriented therapies that stress action in the present rather than analysis of the past.

William Glasser's Reality Therapy holds that everything we do represents a choice. While there may be understandable reasons why in the past we have made choices that have not fulfilled our needs (reasons such as lack of nurturant relationships and lack of awareness of alternatives), it does not do any good to dwell on those reasons now. Past choices (such as addiction or criminal activity) are accepted as "givens"; they cannot be changed now. The obstacles we face in the present are also "givens." Neither past nor present disadvantages absolve us of the responsibility to make choices that "fulfill our needs in a way that does not deprive others of their ability to fulfill their needs."[1] If this sounds like a tough-minded philosophy, it is indeed, but it is also a hopeful one. For if people have the responsibility to choose, they also have the capacity to choose. Anyone has the capacity for growth. We all have the capacity to give up destructive or self-destructive habits, even if we have not had enough support to be able to do so in the past. With the help of the kind of involved therapeutic relationship Glasser recommends, we will be more likely to accept reality and make choices that are responsible as well as realistically attainable.

Jerry read *Reality Therapy* during his first months at Blue Hills. It proved to be a milestone in his recovery.

> When Glasser spoke of total irresponsibility I thought he was writing about me. I learned then that I would have to face things as they had been and as they were, and not blame anything for my fate as I had previously done. That was the bad news. The good news was that I did have some choice, some control over what happened to me. Reading the book was an uncomfortable, disconcerting experience, yet it brought strength to my life.

Jerry had the book with him when he first met Lee. Radiating the assurance of a novice, he intimated that Lee could hardly call himself a counselor if he hadn't read it. Lee rushed out and bought a copy. For him the significance of *Reality Therapy* lay in its presenting A.A.'s Twelve Steps in a different language. "Coming as it did in a context that wasn't specifically connected with drugs or alcohol," he recalls, "the message was very reinforcing as well as broadening."

Rational-Emotive Therapy[2] gives further reinforcement to the message. Starting from essentially the same premises as Glasser, Albert Ellis shows how inaccurate thinking (what A.A. calls "stinking thinking") keeps us from facing reality. Among the many common irrational preoccupations that Ellis exposes are the "musts," "shoulds," and "if onlys" of wishful thinking, which, when it runs up against the way things actually are, becomes self-punishing thinking. People often turn their desires or expectations into demands (e.g., "Everybody should love me all the time"). Only in the artificially secure world of addiction — of unreality — can such demands be consistently met. By bringing us face to face with long-ingrained habits of thought, Rational-Emotive Therapy helps us stop making demands on reality and start taking responsibility for making the choices that reality poses.

In order to make choices that will fulfill our needs, we must first make value judgments. "Do I want to be forty pounds overweight?" "Am I contented to keep working at this job?" "Would I rather give up on my marriage or do what has to be done to work things out?" With practice in making such value judgments, we can look realistically at whether we are living in the way we want to live. Sidney Simon's values-clarification exercises[3] confront us with the consequences of our choices and bring into focus the question of whether the choices we live out match our feelings and thoughts.

All three of these approaches to human growth emphasize individual responsibility and choice. For the person who is recovering from addiction, relationships of mutual support and love are essential, but only insofar as they give the person the strength to begin to develop an identity and assume responsibility. Lee did this on his first day of sobriety when he left his wife a note telling her that "this time, if I was going to do something, I was going to do it for me." Jerry did it when he read *Reality Therapy* and decided that, even if most of his fellow counselors went back to using drugs, he had control over whether or not he did the same. Don did it when he resisted the impulse to reach for a drink every time he got up to speak publicly as a rehabilitation counselor. "I learned," he says, "that the things I said and did were in and of me, whether I was using drugs or not. I didn't need drugs or alcohol to bring them out."

***

Addiction grows out of a basic discomfort with oneself. People who choose addiction usually are afraid to be alone, and when they must be alone they seek out their addiction for company, whether that addiction is food, drink, television, or (as we describe in *Love and Addiction*) a lover or series of lovers. When Don gave up heroin, he first had to get to know himself. Here he was, cut off from his "employment" as a drug hustler and from his old companions. In the treatment program he was the only patient. He was alone quite a bit of the time.

> The pace of my life slowed down. As an addict I'd always had to move fast. Activity was my identity. Now I didn't know what to do, where to start. I had to go back to when I was younger and recall what interested me, what I liked to do. All my life I had run through a tunnel, headed straight for the bag of dope; now I could look around. I enjoyed just sitting down in a restaurant with a cup of coffee and watching the people go in and out. For the first time I felt a part of things and began to identify with the average working person. Instead of a morning wake-up I'd feel good seeing the same waiters and waitresses, the same customers each morning.

Rebirth often begins with a pause for reflection. Such a pause can be very helpful in that it breaks the momentum of the addictive ratrace and lets the recovering person start out in a new, freely chosen direction. Just as Lee could stop and reflect while his business was being liquidated, Don, too, was now out of business.

Slowly Don built up his life. He spent time with his mother, who lived with the constant fear that he would die young, and tried to ease her mind. He brought more people into his life by going out and finding work. This time he didn't talk about his convenient "disability," and when his employer's found out about it he confronted it directly. "What do you want?" he asked them. "Somebody to do the job on time or somebody from the Catholic Church?" And with a job came a wallet, mail, credit cards — expression of people's confidence and tokens of a new identity.

About a year after Don entered treatment, things picked up at Blue Hills. More drug users were taking advantage of the new alternative to prison, and the groups were beginning to show real interchange and energy. For Don it was not all easy. The self-revelation entailed by the group process was difficult and painful, as it is for him even now.

> I was forced to confront a whole period in my life that I wanted to glide over. I didn't want to look at those ten years. In groups, when people would bring up certain incidents, I'd catch myself saying, "Yeah, me too," without really going into it. The memory was still so vivid then; just thinking about it put me right back into that period, back even to my first shot. It was like a madness I'd been through.

In those early years of recovery Don clearly was on an upward path.

> I pursued being clean; I pursued changing my life; I pursued understanding. I made sure I never came under any suspicion of being out on the street fooling around again. I established good relationships with the nurses and staff. I saw the rehabilitation program beginning to develop, and I wanted to get in on the ground floor. I could see ahead — not that far, but maybe six months to a

year ahead at each step of the way.

While no match for Jerry as a hustler, Don was sufficiently street-wise to know that no job opportunities available to him on the "outside" could compare with the prospect of state employment as a drug rehabilitation counselor. Here was a field in which his experience gave him some credentials. That prospect became a reality when psychiatrist Donald Pet came to Blue Hills from Lexington to direct the program. From Lexington Dr. Pet brought innovative treatment methods derived from Reality Therapy rather than the medical-psychoanalytic model, along with a group of drug-free addicts to staff the program as counselors. For Don, who by now had quite a head start on his fellow patients, it was a small step from being intensely involved in the groups to becoming a counselor himself.

While Don established himself in his new career (and at the outset there was no one who did so with greater energy and dedication), he was expanding his personal world as well. Looking back at his years of running down a dark alley, he says, "It's like on a camping trip when you're fogged in for a few days, and then one morning the fog clears, and you can see to move on. I had been fogged in for ten years." The worlds that opened up for him included photography and the outdoors, two interests that went well together.

> I like to go off with a camera and get into nature or into people. Photography has helped me appreciate the aesthetics of things I used to run by and never see — a tree, a barn, a ploughshare in a field, people's faces. With people it has shown me that if you look long enough you can find beauty even in what appears to be ugly. I've taken an hour or two to get to know a person before taking that person's picture. I still correspond with some families in Newfoundland whose pictures I've taken when I visited there. They know nothing about my past; they just take me for who I was when we laughed and had a drink together.

Photography clearly has touched Don deeply. There are photographs he has taken that he keeps privately and does not display. These are portraits of people he has worked with as a counselor, portraits that show, he feels, the kind of pain that he himself has been through.

As Don ranged farther from home on his camping trips, his need for a daily dose of methadone became inconvenient. In 1973, more than five years after he gave up heroin, he decided to give up methadone as well. By now, he thought, there was enough purpose and enough caring in his life to bring him through the discomfort of withdrawal.

> There was also a reward awaiting me — a trip to Newfoundland that I'd planned. If I wanted to get away, I would have to come off methadone. When I did come off, I wasn't exactly ready to go to Newfoundland. I didn't even want to go across the street. But time healed the pain within a few weeks. When I got to Newfoundland I was forced to function — drive for miles and miles, put up tents in the rain, cook, wash in the stream. No nurse was going to do those things for me out there. Within a week I had been so busy and so involved in that environment that I forgot what I had left behind.

Only he had to go back to it all; his vacation couldn't last forever. The problem with using a "reward" like the Newfoundland trip as an incentive to come off methadone was that he thereby made his freedom from the drug contingent on the good feelings that came from being away from the normal stresses of his job and his life. If he was going to surrender the methadone, he would have to surrender it unconditionally, without measuring the rewards at that time or later. He would have to be able to have faith that the strengthened foundation of his life would support him in those moments (which he, like anyone else, would have) when he didn't feel so good. This apparently, he could not do.

In a matter of months he was back on methadone. Time had not healed all the pain.

Lee, too, suddenly had a lot of time on his hands.

> When you come off spending twelve hours a day in a bar, that's a lot of time to fill. Each A.A. meeting you go to is three hours filled, and sometimes you go to two a day. That takes care of the time until you learn to deal with it yourself. By going to those meetings you learn that you can spend your time with people instead of with drugs or alcohol. When I first got sober, if Doris didn't have dinner on the table at five o'clock, I'd be coming out of my skin. That was the old need for instant gratification. Then five-fifteen got to be okay, then five-thirty, and now if it's not on the table until seven o'clock I still have plenty to do.

He soon found that "there weren't enough hours in the day to read, to learn, to love as much as I wanted to" — especially when he had lost so many years.

> For years I had been like Ishmael at the beginning of *Moby Dick,* pausing before coffins, trailing behind funerals, pursuing death. Now I discovered that I wanted to live. Death can be a very disturbing prospect when you have plans for your life and a list of ten books waiting to be read. At a poetry reading I heard a line that went like this: "The heart at times is bloodied by razor-like memories." I could not change those memories. I could only live in the here and now, not the there and then. I couldn't catch up on what I had missed, but I could make sure I wasn't going to miss any more.

The new life that rushed in to fill Lee's time was what constituted his rebirth.

> A spirit of change and growth spread over my life

and affected all my habits, large and small. Every day the old, ingrained routine crumbled up and faded away, and a new world grew up in its place. One life ended, and a second life began. I was reborn.

I went to hear Beethoven; where had he been all my life? I went to a poetry reading — me, at a *poetry reading?* I'm the guy who couldn't hear, couldn't concentrate, couldn't understand. All I'd ever thought about was the bar I'd hit afterward. On my first sober New Year's Eve Doris and I went to Rumpelmeyer's in New York and had ice cream sundaes. I mean, ice cream sundaes; it was crazy! And wow, to find out that music makes sense even if you're not smashed. Music, sex, movies, conversation — things that I could not have imagined without alcohol. I sat in Lincoln Center watching plays, opera, ballet and thought of the nearby bars that I used to pass out in. I used to go down to New York a lot, but I never saw New York, because I went straight from the bar on the train to the bar on the street. Now I saw New York, and I found out that the food there tasted pretty good.

How can I convey the full difference between a normal day or week before and after my rebirth? Now I could travel relaxed and enjoy new sights and sounds. I could eat in restaurants alone. I could have dinner with my wife and converse and remember what I ate. I could go through weekends and holidays consciously and without agony. I could have fun celebrating Christmas while knowing that I could love all year round.

I could get up in the morning and brush my teeth and hug my wife instead of the toilet bowl. I could get up and look out at the sun and feel great — or at least feel tired and not knocked out. I could go to sleep at night without waking up with

> that terror, that pounding heartbeat at three A.M. (as in Robert Frost's poem, "I Have Known the Night"). If I did wake up during the night I could just go to the bathroom and go back to sleep. And if occasionally I couldn't get back to sleep, well, didn't other people have to miss a night's sleep once in a while?

Just as one is born into an imperfect world, so it is when one is reborn. As Lee says, "I had bad days and good days, bad feelings and good feelings. But I had feelings now, and I knew the difference." Now Lee was strong enough to begin to express both his positive and negative feelings. He could face and deal with the areas of personal growth that had (and have) always given him difficulty: his sensitivity to criticism, his fear of confrontations, his wariness of open communication, his unwillingness to admit error. He could take risks. As for drinking, it never again became an issue, even in his bad moments.

> Once I awoke with tears streaming down my face from a dream in which I had been drinking again. It was so real I could taste the liquor. I was so panicky, so remorseful that you would swear I had actually been drunk. I don't think there was even one time when I really did want a drink. But a couple of times when I had been under heavy emotional strain I could sit back and taste that drink oozing down my throat, feeling the fire going through every part of my body, relaxing me. But who was I kidding? I knew that that was not an alternative. That would be death.

If drinking was no longer an issue, *not* drinking was becoming less of an issue as well. In early recovery a person whose life has been predicated on one relationship, one experience, will inevitably be preoccupied with rejecting that relationship and that experience. At that stage someone like Lee who defined himself by his drinking will define himself by his sobriety; someone like Don or Jerry who lived to shoot dope will live to save the souls of addicts. That is the first, but only the first step in recovery. A true rebirth takes a person altogether beyond the fixation on what once was addiction — beyond daily A.A. meetings, beyond drug counseling, beyond the exclusive association with fellow addicts (even recovering addicts). It is an outward movement, a receptiveness to much more in life than the compulsive negation of past compulsions. This outward movement is embodied in the Twelve Steps of A.A.

Addiction means having only one (albeit strongly reinforced) connection with the world; the breaking of that connection is withdrawal. The real antithesis of addiction is a life in which one is tied to others and to reality by many threads. Recovery is a gradual process of building up those "lifelines." Typically, a recovering person first discovers himself by learning to spend time alone, and then discovers that there is more to the world than himself and more to life than being alone.

"As I opened my eyes," says Lee, "my life started to fill out." Whereas Don and Jerry had to build up their new lives from scratch (especially Jerry, since Don had his mother close by), Lee already had a loving family. All he really had to do, as he says, was to open his eyes wide enough to see that they had been there all along. He came to realize that he had been inaccessible to his children as his father had been to him. They had missed him, and he had missed them.

> On my first sober Labor Day I heard Amy, my youngest, who was then about ten years old, pestering her mother to play checkers with her. When Doris suggested that she ask me instead, Amy said, "Daddy doesn't know how to play checkers." "Of course he does," said Doris, and Amy finally came over and had a really enjoyable game of checkers with me.

Lee extended himself in other directions as well. He collected classical music recordings, took courses at the Greater Hartford Council on Alcoholism, and read inspirational religious writers such as Father John Powell and Father Henri Nouwen. Rod McKuen's work introduced him to a new world of love and warmth and optimism. These writers were among his first "gurus," a term he defines as "a teacher, a guide, a significant person in my life who has helped me to learn to become myself." Other early (as well as present) gurus were fellow members of A.A. Later, when Lee started working at Blue Hills and going through bibliographies to obtain more knowledge in the field, his gurus came to include his mentors in counseling and the human growth movement. William Glasser, Albert Ellis, Sidney Simon, Clark Moustakas, Joel Fort, and Sheldon Kopp are among the "cafeteria of gurus" he salutes in *Consider the Alternative.*

Meanwhile, as he was liquidating his business and working on his sobriety, Lee had a chance to reflect about what he wanted to do with his life. Although he did not doubt that he could maintain his sobriety while remaining in the field of business, he sensed that "I needed and wanted to lead a completely different life in sobriety from the life I had led in alcoholism." What prospect of continuing to face the moral dilemmas that, with his newfound honesty, he discerned in his past business practices. Now that he had been exposed to a world of higher ideals and more positive feelings, he wanted these to be reflected in his profession. Besides, he notes,

> In fifteen years in business I never really enjoyed it. I am not a business person. I don't like the bargaining; I don't like what I am selling; I don't like the figures; I don't like the administration. The only part I like is really just being with people and moving and motivating them.

Now that he was free to listen to his feelings, he thought he could strengthen his recovery by doing something that made him happy rather than discontented. His going into counseling was a natural outgrowth of his work in A.A. as well as his reading in the field. Ironically, all the vocational aptitude tests he had taken in high school and college had indicated that he should go into social work, not business. Here was a place where he could put all his energies into "being with people and moving and motivating them."

> I welcomed the challenge of redirecting the very techniques of deviance — the energy, the intensity, the shrewdness, the ability to reach people on their own level and "sell" them something — into a positive force, spreading nourishment and understanding rather than destruction.

When he had been sober for about nine months, Lee applied for a job in alcoholism counseling at Blue Hills Hospital, which offered the best training in the field in the Hartford area. After three months of volunteer work he was hired.

Lee sums up his rebirth in a way that is as readily understandable to a smoker, overeater, or clinging lover as to an alcoholic.

> The problem was never booze, and it was never drugs. The problem was living, and that's the problem today. Like Don and Jerry I was chasing the perfect peace of mind that no one else has. I was once committed to the reduction of anxieties, but I have now learned to tolerate anxieties. I once sought perfect happiness and comfort; now I can be satisfied with reasonable happiness and comfort. I have learned that it's okay to fall, to be hurt, to feel inadequate, to fail — as long as I can rise again, risk again, risk involvement and responsibility, cope without chemicals.
>
> In order to grow, I had to rid myself of all the tyrants — the tyrants of expectation and self-betrayal, the chronic anticipations, the slush fund of anger. I needed kindness and courage, challenge and love. I had to have a sense of meaning, of belief, of commitment, of belonging. I found help by listening and caring and giving and revealing. I found that I was valuable because

> I needed people and people needed me. And so I keep what I've learned by giving it away to as many people as I can.

***

For Jerry to ask for a job as a counselor at Blue Hills right after he got out of Woodbourne (and immediately got high again) was about as absurd as getting a criminal commitment instead of a long jail sentence. But in 1970 Jerry's street background constituted just the kind of credentials Blue Hills was looking for in a counselor. With Donald Pet as chief of professional services, Blue Hills was innovating aggressively in an area where previous forms of treatment had not been very successful. Addicts just recently off the streets themselves, alcoholics with a few months' sobriety, became counselors for, in Jerry's words, "people we were one step ahead of." For Jerry "it was another survival act. Again I had to have my wits about me to survive."

This approach to treatment was based on the belief that the patients and counselors, having similar backgrounds and experiences, would interact in an atmosphere of honesty, empathy, and respect. Indeed, the patients and the counselors (who were themselves regarded as quasi-patients and given urinalyses) did develop a closeness and camaraderie from which the professionals were excluded. The counselors acted as advocates for the patients, who were there for detoxification, methadone maintenance, or residential treatment. They made referrals and interceded on the patients' behalf with the courts, schools, and the departments of welfare and vocational rehabilitation.

For a while it worked. The counselors hardly knew what they were doing, but they worked with a contagious enthusiasm that got results. For the first time some of the addict or alcoholic patients felt that someone was reaching out to them on their own level, as one human being to another. Whether Jerry or Lee or Don knew the appropriate counseling techniques didn't seem to matter. Each of them has since had someone come up to him — someone he may not even recognize — and thank him for "saving my life seven or eight years ago at Blue Hills."

It worked for Jerry, too, who with no formal background was running two or three groups a day.

> Blue Hills was a uniquely valuable experience. Even with the administrative hassles and personality conflicts, it gave me just what I needed at the time — a bit of structure, a bit of autonomy. It provided some discipline along with a group that I could identify positively with. Nowhere else did I get the training I got there.

Jerry needed more than a job; he needed an all-around support system. The only family he had in the Hartford area was his two young sons, who lived with his estranged wife. Now he could be a father to them for the first time. But he still needed a place to live. The state put him up in the Compass Club, a halfway house adjacent to Blue Hills, and gave me a $39.50-a-month living allowance as a counselor trainee. He was a staff member and yet was considered to be in therapy twenty-four hours a day.

At first, like Lee and Don, Jerry wondered how he was going to fill those twenty-four hours.

> When Don and I had just started out as counselors, he came over one Sunday morning at eight, and we drove around all day in his little sports car. Somehow we just didn't hit it off, but we just kept driving around together because that was all we had to keep busy with that day. Thank God when the day was over and we could get ready for work the next morning.

Horrifying as this story may sound to those who know the value of gasoline in the 1980s, at the time it was a better choice than getting high again. As the weeks went on Jerry found another alternative that was even better. Still afraid that in some unstructured moment he might fall back into the abyss he had just climbed out of, he threw himself into his job and into his relationships with the counselors he worked with at Blue Hills and lived with at the Compass Club. These were hard-core drug and alcohol users who had come off the streets via Lexington. They were Jerry's peers in age and experience. There was no way he could call them "faggots."

With his verbal skills, Jerry was an immediate success as a group leader. Still, as the first person without a Lexington background to break into the counseling group at Blue Hills, he felt that he had some catching up to do. So he took a course in introductory psychology at the University of Hartford. That gave him six college credits. It is here that Lee tells "Abe Lincoln stories" about Jerry walking or hitchhiking five or six miles in the snow to get to the University. "He'd always be conning somebody," Lee recalls, "usually somebody quite attractive, into giving him a ride."

A formative influence on Jerry was his friendship with Tom Verner, a Peace Corps veteran ten years Jerry's junior and the first counselor at Blue Hills who did not himself have a history of addiction. It was Tom who introduced Jerry and Lee to existential philosophy and the modern theater. At Blue Hills Jerry staged a production of Sartre's *No Exit,* with patients acting the parts. Tom also encouraged Jerry to accelerate his college course schedule and taught him to be more pragmatic in his dealings with patients and the administration. According to Jerry,

> Co-leading groups with Tom was an education in subtlety. I have a straightforward, perhaps aggressive approach to most things. I put my head down and plow right through. Tom taught me that it's sometimes more effective to coopt people than to bang them over the head.

At meetings Jerry sometimes acted out, cursing and pounding his fist. At other times he was tactful and conciliatory. "As at other institutions," he says, "I learned what I had to do."

Jerry remembers this early period at Blue Hills as a happy one, full of the excitement of self-discovery.

> What with my work, my living situation, my outside reading and studies, all my needs were being filled at Blue Hills and the related milieu that made up my social environment. Meetings, courses, books, discussions, groups — if there was something happening, I wanted to be there. It was like a new territory where I didn't speak the language and didn't have a guidebook, yet I saw opening out before me a clear prospect of success.

As Jerry put some distance between himself and his last bag of dope, things began to move a lot faster for him.

> I moved out of the Compass Club and into Don's apartment complex in East Hartford. I went to the theater and read as much Shakespeare as I could. I discovered that I could go out and hold my own in conversation. I got involved with women who had never been addicts. I spent as much time as I could with my two boys, taking them to ballgames or to Lee's summer house on Columbia Lake.

After Jerry was divorced from his first wife, Doris Silverstein introduced him to a good friend of hers, a teacher and educational consultant named Chris, who was twelve years younger than he and a person of great insight and sensitivity. Jerry and Chris both stood at pivotal moments in their careers, and the strength and responsibility they showed toward each other drew them together in a union of honesty and mutual support. In June, 1972, on the day after the Watergate burglary, they were married in a rose garden in Elizabeth Park. Tom Verner, who had moved to British Columbia, flew in for the wedding and wrote a poem in honor of the occasion. For their honeymoon the couple took a camping trip to eastern Canada, with evenings at the theater in Montreal and Quebec City.

It was two and half years since Jerry had come out of Woodbourne.

8
reality

The world of the recovering person is not a pain-free paradise. On the contrary, paradise is the false promise of addiction. Looking back at the years he spent drowning his pain in booze, Lee reflects, "What did the earth people do when they got a bad grade or lost a business deal? There were people out there facing these things. Why was I the only one who wasn't supposed to suffer?" When Lee says, "Every sober day I've had — even the ones most full of sorrow — has been better than any day when I was drunk," he means that it is better to live and sometimes suffer than to deny suffering through a kind of death. Suffering is part of living — this is the first lesson that the recovering person learns. So you're off drugs (or whatever). Big deal. Welcome to the land of ulcers, marital problems, deaths in the family, hassles on the job.

Winston Churchill said that success is never final, failure never fatal. Neither of these truths may be readily apparent to the coordinator at Daytop Village or Synanon who, after being responsible for three hundred people at the concept house, comes out into the "real world" and is told to pick up a broom. It is natural for the recently drug-free addict to think, "I'm a counselor — I'm going to be a big success!" or "Nobody offered me a job this week — I'm the same failure I always was." It is natural for the recovering person who does get a job to start wondering, "Is this all there is to it? I have to work eight hours a day just to come home and hear my wife and kids yelling?"

'Hey, look at me!" you exclaim when you kick the habit, as if the world is going to stop and tip its hat to you. Instead of hearing bells ring all over the city you feel lousy, don't sleep for a week, miss three days of work, and catch hell from your boss. Then you have to start making the same choices everyone else does — choices about how to live with the pain and how to cope with it. The bells are going to have go off inside you.

***

Jerry's progress at Blue Hills had not been altogether as smooth as it might have seemed on the sunny day in the rose garden when he got married. The tight, sometimes unholy coalition between patients and counselors, together with Jerry's persistent doubts about himself and his recovery, created situations in which he compromised himself. "Clients would come in with shirts, ties, jackets, even a radio or stereo," he recalls, "and I bought a few of these things without asking many questions." Early in 1971 he was suspended for six weeks for having sex with a woman patient. The medical director, the late Dr. Eugene Rosenfeld, told him, "That's what we do with you fellas. If someone else did this, we'd can him." After his reinstatment Jerry kept his nose clean. Not that he had done anything wrong, of course. He just didn't want to lose his job.

> Six months later I asked Dr. Rosenfeld to clarify what he had said to me. He replied, "This isn't any career that you fellas have here. We're just paying you some money so you won't take drugs. You can't support a family as a patient-counselor. The job is just meant to be a springboard back into the larger community. The reason we only suspend you when you break the rules is that we expect you fellas to do that. We expect you to take a state

> car on Thursday and bring it back Monday all smashed up. We knew when we brought you here that that would happen. Then he added, "But I understand that you're going to school. Keep it up."
>
> That speech made it clear to me where I stood as one of "you fellas." It lit up both paths for me — the one going backward and the one going forward. I was very much afraid of losing my job. What was I going to do — sell shoes again? But I also saw that in taking those college courses I might be headed somewhere. Since I was going to school and spending time with people who didn't use drugs, since I was now getting knowledge and support from other sources than the group at Blue Hills, I saw that I didn't have to follow suit when other counselors started to use drugs again. I didn't have to continue receiving stolen goods and fooling around with women patients. I could make my own choices.

Jerry believes that the recovering addict invariably must choose, as he did, between two paths — "the one going backward and the one going forward." There is no middle ground. "You can't go on feeling good about yourself just because you aren't using drugs anymore. That alone won't hold you. Either you move on, or you'll tend to go back the other way. But if you do move on, you move into a different world. Everything around you changes."

Jerry here is speaking of what Lee calls "plateaus of growth." An alcoholic who after five years of sobriety keeps going to A.A. meetings every night and telling everyone, "I'm clean, I'm sober," is stuck at an initial plateau. Further growth, which A.A.'s Twelve Steps encourage, entails greater involvement with work, family, friendships, insight therapy, or whatever adds new meaning, support, and satisfaction to the person's life.

This is how Jerry describes some of his own early plateaus:

> It was one thing to stop using drugs. It was another thing to stop abusing my position and conniving with patients because I didn't want to lose my job and go back to jail. And it was another thing altogether when I could go into a department store and not even feel the impulse to steal something. Or when I became genuinely concerned that there be money in my account to cover any check I wrote. Or when I made a point of honoring every commitment I made to be at a certain place at a certain time. By then I had found a way to feel good about myself by making my word, my presence mean something.

Speaking of himself and his friends, Jerry says,

> A long time ago we got onto a conveyor belt going the wrong way: you don't develop skills, you hang out with drug users, you get high, you get busted, you go to jail, you become ineligible for jobs, you go back to the old crowd, you get high again...It was very difficult to get off that conveyor belt, but when we did, we stayed off it by getting on a conveyer going the opposite direction. When Lee ran to every meeting in the Hartford area having to do with alcohol and drugs, when Don threw himself into involvement with the patients at Blue Hills, when I walked back and forth to the University in the snow, we were creating a foundation for ourselves. We didn't know we were building it; it was a subtle, insidious process.
>
> When I signed up for Psychology 110 in the summer of 1970, I didn't think those three credits would change my life significantly. But that course put me on a conveyor belt that brought me to many other nice places and took me far away from drug use. When I was in the street, my friends were drug addicts, hustlers — people like

> myself. When I came to Blue Hills, my friends were counselors, ex-addicts — people like myself. Now my friends are social workers, psychologists, professionals — people like myself. I didn't plan it that way. It's just that I associate with people with whom I have things in common, and I come to have things in common with the people with whom I associate.

A plateau which Jerry reached on the way to this professional status was his decision to leave his job at Blue Hills and go to school full-time. Watching Lee simultaneously working at Blue Hills and taking a master's degree at the University of Connecticut School of Social Work, Jerry realized that he needed credentials to progress in the field. Strongly encouraged by Lee and by Chris, whom he had just married, he set out to complete his undergraduate education at Eastern Connecticut State College in Willimantic.

***

In 1974, when he had been away from Blue Hills for a couple of years, Jerry came back to visit some of the counselors he had worked with there.

> Out of about twenty-five co-workers that I had known at this state facility, only two or three were still there. What had happened to the rest? Some were in treatment programs for themselves for drugs or alcoholism. Some were in jail. One or two may have been in school. Some were just floundering. Some had simply disappeared.

What happened? Trying to make sense of his observations, Jerry began to review his own experiences as a counselor. He saw that in his two and half years on the job he had gone through four "stages of disillusionment." The first stage was *enthusiasm,* in which his fervent belief in what he was doing more than compensated for his lack of knowledge in enabling him to work effectively with clients. Long hours, low pay, lack of status and power on the job, lack of time and opportunity for fulfillment off the job — these issues did not matter. All that mattered was that he was helping people, "curing" people. His job was his life.

The second stage, *stagnation*, occurred when other needs made themselves felt. Now it was no longer enough to be saving the world; he wanted an apartment, a car, a personal and social life. As a paraprofessional counselor he wouldn't be able to have these. Nor could he gain the respect of the professionals with whom he worked, even though it was he who was out there on the front lines working with addicts. Jerry recalls a clinical conference at which a scribe took notes while a psychiatrist, a nurse, and a social worker reported on a patient's case. When Jerry rose to speak as the patient's counselor, the scribe went to the bathroom.

Once Jerry got a letter from a former client which said, "You changed my life." Jerry carried the letter around with him for weeks — until he read in the newspaper that the man had been convicted of armed robbery. As he came to question whether he was doing anybody any good, he entered the third stage — *frustration.* He felt powerless, overworked, put upon, hassled, unappreciated not only by superiors but by clients as well.

As stagnation and frustration settled in among the counselors, the men whom Jerry had once looked upon as models of enthusiasm came to project a very different image. Now he would see them laughingly drink a bottle of gin (followed by chewing gum, cigarettes, and mouthwash) to fortify themselves for a group meeting with their clients. It was in that atmosphere that Jerry (although he did not abuse alcohol or resume narcotic use as others did) felt entitled to come to work late, take long lunches, neglect his paperwork, receive stolen goods, have affairs with woman clients. In a natural reaction to frustration, he and his fellow counselors had come full circle from dedication to indifference. This was the fourth stage, *apathy,* where "a job is a job is a job."

When Jerry developed the concept of "stages of disillusionment," he assumed that it applied mainly to overworked, underpaid front-line paraprofessionals. He was in for a surprise. With increased exposure to the human services field, first as a student and then as a teacher, he has learned that anyone who works with people is susceptible to what has come to be known as job burnout. Burnout is now a major concern not only in the helping professions, but in business and industry as well. By virtue of his baptism of fire in the drug counseling milieu, Jerry has been in an ideal position to observe the more subtle manifestations of burnout in nurses, schoolteachers, psychologists, psychiatrists, welfare caseworkers, family and correctional counselors, and human service administrators. He has seen the attitudes of enthusiasm, stagnation, frustration, and apathy being passed on from helper to helper and from helper to client. He has seen the cycle of unrealistic expectations and disillusionment repeat itself several times over the course of a person's career. And he has seen the effects of burnout: alcohol abuse, headaches, ulcers, backaches, sexual problems, broken marriages, interrupted careers, abandoned ambitions.

In his workshops and in *Burnout: Stages of Disillusionment in the Helping Professions,*[1] Jerry demonstrates that one can intervene effectively against burnout by enlarging one's personal and professional world. Like Lee, Jerry has accomplished this in part through further education. He earned his M.S.W. degree at the University of Connecticut School of Social Work in 1976, as Lee had done three years earlier. (Lee still remarks on the way the professionals at Blue Hills all called him "Mr. Silverstein" until the day he got his degree; after that day they called him "Lee.") Since then, Jerry has sought to avoid stagnation by moving into such areas as gerontology, youth services, human sexuality, family therapy, and staff development. Having sensed that he was burning out as a front-line "helper," he has created a new career for himself as a teacher and consultant, "working with the people who work with people."

Intervening against burnout is a form of problem-solving. As Jerry and Lee stress in their workshops, problem-solving means choosing between doing something and doing nothing. Doing something involves risk. When Jerry started college in his mid-thirties, he had no idea what college was. He was older than the rest of the students and had never gone to high school. He knew that he might sound stupid in class. He might stick out like a sore thumb. But he was willing to check it out, to take the plunge. He saw that he had more to gain than to lose.

Doing nothing has consequences as well. Don chose not to resume his education and earn professional status. Instead, he remained a counselor at Blue Hills for ten years. In *Burnout* Jerry asks people how they would feel if they found themselves working at the same job ten years later. The interviewees, most of whom have better jobs than Don, give answers like these: "I'd kill myself!" "The pits!" "I'd be drunk!" "No way!" "Like a caged animal!" Don actually lived out these prophecies of apathy. There he was, ten years later, with his champagne taste on a beer budget, still working at the job that was Jerry's paradigm case of burnout, a job at which most counselors lasted for at most two or three years before moving on to greater responsibilities or back out on the street. Don tried to make a life out of a job that was intended as an initial opportunity, a rope thrown out to a drowning man.

It didn't work for several reasons. The turnover rate being what it was, Don did not have a stable group of friends among his fellow counselors. Each year or two he saw a new group of counselors pass by on one of Jerry's two "conveyor belts" — up and out or (in most cases) down and out. Either way it was discouraging for him — most of all, perhaps, when Lee and Jerry left Blue Hills for better opportunities. Moreover, in the course of the decade it became harder for Don or anyone else to work effectively with addicts in confrontative, jive-talking style that was the "patient-counselor's" stock in trade. "At the beginning," Lee recalls, "no one loved that job more or gave more hours or cared less about money than Don. No one could maintain the pace he did." No one, not even Don. For things were changing; the counselor no longer had the upper hand. Now the addict did not face a long jail term (thank goodness) as the only alternative to accepting the discipline of the program. Addicts found that they could go from one clinic to another to get what they wanted. Addicts coming in from affluent communities displayed a self-assurance unknown to the previous generation of clinic patients. Young polydrug users (LSD, speed) were showing up with new forms of "jive" that caught the addict-counselor unaware. As Jerry puts it, one reason he left Blue Hills was that "I had gotten too far away from the addict on the street to be able to reach common ground with him."

Then, too, as the spirit of innovation at the program faded, Don became increasingly troubled by what he saw as the careerist mentality of some professional staff members. As he recalls,

> When I'd see somebody not miss a beat in eating his dinner after hearing that one of our clients had just died, I'd ask myself, "Is this what it's turned into?" While I was concerned that an addict we were working with was going to die if we didn't do something for him fast, somebody else would be concerned about the paper she was writing about that person. Then when he did die, she'd say, "I'm still going to present my paper; it took me five days of work." Now, I'm not making myself out to be some altruistic saint. It's just that I was put in a position where I *had* to care, *had* to have feelings. Maybe I'm naive, but if that's the way it's going to be, don't put me out on the front lines to form relationships with people and than pass my notes on to someone else to make decisions about their lives. Let me do some other work, let me put together educational films, but don't put me in direct daily contact with someone who's in need and then make me go through channels.

What the counselor needed now, both to be able to do the job well and to gain respect and decision-making power in doing it, was not just "street credentials," but skill development.

In an era guided by the "Proposition 13 mentality," the addict-counselor has lost credibility. Society will not so readily indulge people who drink on the job, have affairs with patients, traffic in stolen goods, go joyriding in state cars, and perhaps use heroin on the side. The current trend is to hire non-addicts with college degrees, who are less likely to do these things, and to qualify ex-addicts only after they have gone through the same rigorous training as everyone else. The Blue Hills program itself is being reorganized along these lines.

Looking back at Don's experience as well as his own, Jerry has concluded that to hire drug-free addicts and recovering alcoholics as counselors before they have had a chance to create other options for themselves is usually a misguided kindness. If a person is given a counseling job solely on the basis of negative "credentials," then that person will inevitably be patronized by the professional staff. As Don says, "When the people who give you your paycheck can make you take a urinalysis any time they want, after a while even getting the paycheck can become degrading."

Furthermore, if the counseling job is the only non-menial job available to the person, then the job will be, as the drug or alcohol once was, a dependency. Recovering persons probably would be better served by being asked — and given opportunities — to develop strength in other areas before being accepted as counselors. Working in the private sector, taking an associate's degree, exploring personal involvements, doing supervised volunteer work — any or all of these can be effective before-the-fact interventions against burnout for the addiction counselor.

***

If doing nothing, as Don learned, doesn't solve any problems, what about doing something? It may indeed solve some problems, although there are no guarantees. But as numerous case illustrations in *Burnout* reveal, new problems (or the same problems in a different guise) can always crop up. There are no permanent interventions; problem-solving is an ongoing process.

Lee, for example, has never been one for doing nothing. He is always doing things, the right things; working, getting an education, expanding his horizons and helping others do the same. There is, however, one thing his "can do" mentality cannot do, and that is to smooth out the path that lies ahead of him.

In his first years of recovery, while he was discovering new worlds of involvement and satisfaction in A.A. and at Blue Hills and the School of Social Work, Lee was having trouble sorting out his personal life. He was up against what was called "the issue that's never talked about" — at least until *Love and Addiction,* which showed that sex and drugs can substitute for each other as addictions, and Jon Weinberg's *Sex and Recovery,* which explored the way relationships can be disrupted as well as transformed when one partner begins to experience sex with a consciousness newly liberated from addiction.[2]

Lee, who for twenty years had never thought of having sex without alcohol, discovered "a whole new world of pleasure" once he got over his initial fears. For several years, in his own words, he "acted like a nineteen-year-old kid." He turned to sex — a way of getting high on people — as a substitute for the alcohol "high." It was a natural thing to do while he was just beginning to build a new life and find inner meanings.

For Lee, having an affair was the "high" at the end of the day. As he progressed in recovery and developed his integrity in other areas, he was able to question whether his dishonesty toward women (including, of course, his wife) was consistent with his new, responsible life. He saw that he was using his outside sexual "highs," like his work "high," to evade the issues he needed to deal with at home. As Jerry, who went through similar experiences, puts it,

> Whether sex is or is not an addiction depends, as with anything else, on the individual's relationship with it. When I was addicted to drugs I used sex in much the same way — to get high. When I stopped indulging in drugs I began to relate differently to sex as well. I stopped keeping score, stopped putting notches in my belt. I

> began to view women in a different light. As with drugs, the way I approach sex depends on what's going on in my life overall.

While Lee was having his affairs, he was, of course, still "conning" and deceiving Doris, his wife. Previously he had claimed that he was working late when he was actually going off to bars; now he was "working late" to cover for his rendezvous with women. As much as Lee wanted to have his relationship with Doris reflect his newfound honesty (which would have been in keeping with her values as well), he and she were largely unable to break the destructive patterns they had formed over twenty years. During those years Doris hadn't left Lee because her traditional upbringing had made it difficult for her to consider that alternative, especially when Lee continued to support the family and did not physically abuse her or the children. Instead, she retreated into apathy, which Lee calls "the ultimate hostility." After Lee became sober he and Doris, like other couples in similar circumstances, found that "we were locked into the past in ways we were not even aware of."

When Lee replaced nights out at the bar with nights out at A.A. meetings, Doris couldn't have been happier — for about a month. Then she decided that, now that he was "cured," he didn't have to go to any more meetings. Of course, since Lee had several times "gone dry" for longer than a month, Doris had no real reason to believe that he was now sober (and did not in fact believe it for about two years). What she was expressing was her anger at A.A., not only for taking up Lee's time but for doing for him what she tried and failed to do for years. Throughout their entire married life Doris had done everything she could to help Lee stop drinking. Then he went to a few meetings with some strangers, and that did the trick. Such unrecognized frustration and anger regarding A.A. is common among husbands and wives of alcoholics. As for Doris, she only became aware of it several years later in therapy. In the meantime, she and Lee got into pitched battles of the sort that he describes here.

> One Saturday night we blew up. "I'm going to the

> meeting!" I said, and stormed out to the car. Then it dawned on me that she'd never been to a meeting. So I went back up to the house and invited her to come along. As angry as she was, she did come and was quite moved by what she saw. Still, even after that we'd get into arguments over things I felt I had to do for my sobriety, and I'd get as irrational as she would. Finally I'd just say, "Listen, I have to do this for my sobriety. That's what comes first."

Whether it was A.A. or anything else, Lee and Doris "just backed into corners and staked out our positions." In Doris Lee apparently had found someone as stubborn as he was. Neither of them was able to break fresh ground in search of a compromise. When Lee was a few years into his sobriety they separated, with Lee taking over his family's summer house on Columbia Lake as his full-time home. But they didn't really separate. Both of them were always finding pretexts to call or drop by. As Lee says, "We were so bound up with each other; we never stopped loving each other; but we couldn't live together in any but a destructive way — picking at each other, tearing at each other, expecting each other to be perfect even though we couldn't perfect ourselves." After two years of separation their marriage counselor said that both of them were still taking exactly the same positions they had two years earlier. No movement.

Meanwhile, Lee was learning that education and professional credentials are no guarantee against job burnout. While Don was burning out as a paraprofessional counselor, Lee was going through the cycle of disillusionment more than once as a social services administrator. The same thing might just as easily have happened if he had stayed in business. It could happen to a recovering person in any line of work.

When Lee obtained his M.S.W. degree in 1973 he left Blue Hills and became coordinator of the psychiatric day program at Hartford Hospital. Within months he was promoted to Director of Social Services. There he displayed the intolerance that frequently attends the zeal of recovery — in his case not the intolerance of the reformed addict toward follies like his own (for Lee remembers how long it took for him to choose sobriety, and what a miracle it was when he did), but an intolerance toward "helpers" who do not do enough to help. He got into an imbroglio with the social workers he supervised over his conviction that social work is a twenty-four-hour-a-day commitment. Lee believed that someone should always be on call for those who needed help outside of regular hours. But the social workers closed ranks around their nine-to-five schedule. After fourteen months, even though he had the support of the administration, Lee resigned. "I would have won the battle but lost the war," he explains. "With all the conflict, we wouldn't have been helping people." Placed in a position of authority over people who had an independent power base, Lee had been drawn into a conflict over power and control, a futile struggle to force others to live up to his ideals.

Upon his resignation as Director of Social Services, Lee became Director of Alcoholism Services, a new program at the hospital which he himself set up. Here, in an area less governed by bureaucratic tradition, he was able to exert the kind of constructive authority that he felt was needed. Yet once he was no longer plagued by conflicts with subordinates, he got into conflicts with himself. He experienced a form of burnout that is common among people who have been through the energetic pursuit of an addiction: overwork.

Lee had known the strain of overwork when he was a hard-drinking businessman. He had known it when, as a novice social worker, he tried to satisfy his conscience by taking one free client for each paying client. Now he was getting strung out again. Between too much administration and too many outside seminars, he got into a seven-day-a-week work cycle. He was working from 6:30 in the morning to 11:30 at night. He was losing touch with his eating habits, losing touch with his sleep schedule, losing touch with his family responsibilities — the very things he was teaching people to be concerned with. "Just as in the old days," he reflects, "I was using my dedication to work as an excuse to avoid dealing with personal issues."

He wasn't just hurting himself, he felt. He was letting down the people he was trying to help.

> I was losing touch with the caring, losing my primary commitment to the individual addicted person. I became dissatisfied with the clinical treatment I was giving. I was cutting corners, cutting people short on appointments, confronting people too soon, pushing them into alternatives too fast. Outwardly it was all working out. The people didn't object; the administration didn't object. Nobody knew the difference, except me. I felt the difference.
>
> I felt it most strongly in my lectures and workshops, which weren't giving me any satisfaction. It was so mechanical — it was as if there was a tape machine in my throat. I'd go from place to place, and the groups would become a blur. I'd lose track of which thing I said to which group. In the movie *The Turning Point* a ballet star describes her life: "I go from one dance to the next." It was like that for me. I was doing a road show — an hour here, an hour there, never knowing who the people in the audience were. Just like all those songs about one-night stands. Just like all the aimless running I did when I was drinking.
>
> And as with drinking, I felt the loss of the high. The highs I had gotten from alcohol and drugs had lasted a long time at first, but then they got shorter and shorter. Now the same thing was happening with the workshops. I didn't feel any different when one of them ended. I was losing the good work highs with which I had replaced the alcohol and drug highs. It was much like the end of my drinking period, when I'd float through a business meeting and not even know it was happening, or when I'd sit in a bar dreamily contemplating a million-dollar financial collapse.

> I felt that same detachment now. I was almost a bystander, looking on as I gave a lecture. And it scared me to feel that way again.

Lee again realized that, as Sidney Simon puts it, it was time for him to answer to his own value system. He needed to reconcile his actions with his professed beliefs. In February, 1976, Lee's friends received a letter from him announcing that he was leaving his job to take a sabbatical at the Mt. Savior Monastery in the Adirondack Mountains near Elmira, New York. In the letter Lee explained that his desire for an experience of simplicity and reintegration grew out of "memories of the clarity of purpose and absence of complexity that marked the early months of my involvement in the field." In other words, having gone through a cycle of burnout, he wanted to recapture his initial enthusiasm.

Looking back, Lee feels that he did achieve his purpose in going to the monastery.

> Since I don't know how to moderate very well, the only thing I could do was to shut off the pressure entirely for a while, just as I did when I stopped drinking and got out of the business. Taking this sabbatical was the most controversial thing I've ever done. My family, my friends, and the hospital did not want me to do it. But it was probably the smartest single thing I ever did. As one of Ira Progoff's "Stepping Stones," it was a major milestone in my life, almost as significant as sobriety. At the monastery, shoveling cow manure at dawn and reading books that had sat on my shelf for years, I was able to reflect on my priorities and consider my direction. There I recovered my center and regained my purpose.

At the monastery Lee also began to write *Consider the Alternative.* That project and his whole sabbatical were cut short in April with the news that his recently divorced wife Doris had an inoperable brain tumor. Lee at once came back to support Doris through her fatal illness and to see that his children still had a home. In this period of intense pressure and pain, he was thankful to have had the cleansing experience of two months at Mt. Savior.

Doris never wanted the divorce that she and Lee were granted just months before her fatal illness was diagnosed. She was left with the feeling that, after sharing all the bad years with Lee, she was missing out on the good ones. Lee, too, wishes that Doris could be here to share his present fulfillment, although he realistically concedes that he and she probably would not be sharing it as husband and wife. In this frank assessment of his life with Doris he acknowledges her continuing place in his thoughts and feelings.

> Doris used to complain that even when I was with her, I wasn't really with her; I was always attending to something else. But later, when she wasn't with my physically anymore, she remained with me, and still does. The only way I could lose her, the only way I could be free to remarry, was through her death. I never could tell her that I loved her, never could tell her that I needed her, until she was in a coma and could no longer hear me. Doris was honest and direct. She understood a lot more about love than I did, and she could express what she felt. She could tell me that she loved me; she had a sense of commitment; and it frightened me away. She tried to be a part of me, and I shut her out. I continue to live with this knowledge.

That fall Lee completed *Consider the Alternative* with the help of two younger colleagues, Linda Roberts and Jon Brett. He also became Director of Human Services and Alcoholism Services at Rockville Hospital, working with a paraprofessional staff whose commitment did not end at 5 P.M. Although Lee now keeps his life in better balance than he used to, he still has to cope with the impulse to see one more client, visit one more city, do one more workshop, make one more phone call. Two years after his monastic retreat Lee again took a brief respite from his work, this one necessitated by open-heart surgery. The people who know Lee were not surprised to see him go off to do a series of workshops in California when he was barely out of the hospital.

Lee's story illustrates more than one kind of "surrender." When his drinking and drug-taking made him seriously ill or threatened his marriage he would go through periods of what Tiebout calls "submission," or superficial acceptance of situational constraints, as when he would think, "Someday, though maybe not right now, I'll be able to drink again." Then came the deep, unconscious surrender that gave him sobriety; this surrender was genuine, complete, and lasting. Yet, while he has given up alcohol and drugs unconditionally, he is still at times susceptible to the anger, the excessive ambition, and the need for control that were associated with his alcoholism. This is what Tiebout calls "selective surrender."

Lee is aware that "if I see myself bitching and barking at everybody all the time, if I keep acting like I think everybody's out of step but me, then I have to do some examining." He knows that recovery is an ongoing process. In his words,

> Even today I feel some of my old terrors, the "vultures." The idolatry of activism, the chronic anticipation, the fear of other people's reactions, the insistent drumbeat of instant gratification — these are things I am still working on. But now I feel these as a positive challenge to my readiness to hear, to move, and to change; my willingness to risk, to trust, and to give and receive acceptance.

Currently Lee is facing up to the challenge of what is perhaps the most difficult area of living for him, that of maintaining a stable intimate relationship. He remarried a year after Doris' death, and he and his wife Pam have been trying to build upon this fresh start by achieving a level of honesty and sharing that was not possible for Lee in the past. It is still a struggle, and the future continues to bring uncertainties.

Women, love, intimacy, and past failures in relationships continue to pose problems for Lee and for Jerry and Don as well. Jerry is working on his relationships outside of marriage, since he and Chris have been divorced. Their marriage broke down under the pressure of Jerry's overscheduled life and his acknowledged overcommitment to work. Like many other ambitious, career-oriented American males, Jerry did not spend enough time at home to be able to resolve the normal problems that come up in a family. Like Lee, though, Jerry has worked hard to become a good father to his three children (two sons by his first marriage and a daughter by his second). They will have what Jerry did not have — good homes to grow up in and two parents who care about them, even if both parents are not present together.

As for Don, his relationships with women have been a focal point of his emotional vulnerability. His inability to feel easy about his decisions regarding women appears to be one source of the pain that has driven him back to drugs for solace.

9

and then there was one

What happens when Lee and Jerry suffer disappointments? What happens when they fight with their wives or co-workers, or when a workshop that they've put a lot of energy into "bombs"? What happens when it's "just not one of those days"?

What happens is that they have to be about twice as strong as everybody else. Andrew Malcolm, a Canadian physician, has coined the term "chemophilic society"[1] to describe a world in which a variety of intoxicating drugs are made readily available, and people are even encouraged to use them. "Just look around you," says Lee. "You have the singles bars, where everybody has a drink in their hand and some of them are pushing stuff, too. You come home from a rough day at work, and you see everybody popping martinis or beer to 'relax'." Cigarette advertising and models of tobacco use are all around. Food is produced and packaged in unhealthy forms and "pushed" everywhere from supermarkets to movie counters to vending machines, leading to widespread weight and nutritional problems and numerous instances of severe food addiction. Society glorifies romantic love, which then becomes another intoxicant for those in need.

As Jon Weinberg has noted, for most people it is an accepted form of emotional adjustment at some times to use chemicals (or whatever else serves as an intoxicant) in place of internal coping mechanisms. Most people are permitted to overeat occasionally or to come home every day and "simmer down" with a drink. But the person who has identified his or her relationship to, say, alcohol or food as addictive and who has genuinely surrendered the addiction does not have that alternative. (For the food addict the commitment never again to use food addictively is just as rigorous as the alcoholic's commitment never to drink again.) The recovering person, whose emotional adjustment previously was not as good as the average person's, now must aim higher than average. This is part of the miracle of recovery, and of the elusiveness of recovery for many people.

Addiction happens progressively, whether the first time around or in a relapse from apparent recovery. As Donald Pet has told Lee, it would be a short step from saying, "I deserve to take some Valium because of the pressures I'm under from my wife's terminal illness," to deciding, "I deserve it because of the pressures I'm under from a traffic jam." The difference between giving up an addiction unconditionally and giving it up "except in certain circumstances" is the difference between true recovery and an unstable and ultimately unsuccessful recovery.

The hardest thing for a new member of Alcoholics Anonymous or Overeaters Anonymous or a drug addiction group to accept is the idea of *never* taking the drug or addictive object again, never getting high again, never again experiencing those feelings. People look for a catch, an "out," like "One day at a time — I guess that means I can drink on holidays," or "Maybe I'll get high again when I'm sixty-five; the cops won't mess with an old man." It's only natural to think that way when one has been functioning almost entirely through some sort of addictive substitute.

On the other hand, it becomes only natural to think in terms of 'never' when one moves up through the "plateaus of growth" that Lee and Jerry talk about. "If a recovering person has good relationships, dignity, love, a larger purpose, and some fun and relaxation," says Jerry, "then regression to drug use will not become an issue." Jerry learned just how true this is when, after he had been drug-free for five or six years, he was given morphine for painful second-degree burns suffered in a fire that left him and Chris and their infant daughter homeless. "With all my personal and professional knowledge about drugs and drug use," he recalls, "the standard concept of addiction — the popular conception of an all-powerful drug that gains ascendancy over anyone who takes it — had me so propagandized that I had second thoughts about taking morphine when I was lying there in physical pain." In fact, he felt no desire to have another "shot" of morphine the next morning. Nor did he abuse the unlimited supply of percodan pills that had been prescribed for him.

> At the end of a month there was no more pain in my leg, so I stopped taking the percodan. I didn't say to myself, "Well, what the hell, I'll take another two and have myself a little high. It won't hurt anybody." The difference was in what was going on in my life. I had a different relationship with people, with work, with the things that had become important to me.

Those who choose to relapse to addiction are those who have not built up the kind of relationships with people, work, and pleasure that would enable them to change their relationships with alcohol, narcotics, food, cigarettes, lovers, gambling, television, or whatever their "drug" is. As Jerry learned from his experience with morphine.

> You don't just suddenly fall off of the cliff. First you have to put yourself on the edge. I would have to work at relapsing by this point. I would have to begin not paying my bills, not showing up to teach my classes. I would have to let my personal life get slovenly. I would have to undermine the whole life structure.

***

When Don had been at Blue Hills for seven years he was

suspended for three months for unauthorized, non-medical use of the narcotic Dilaudid. Dilaudid was the drug that Don had been getting "under the table" from a doctor just before he entered the methadone program at Blue Hills, and it was to a "no questions asked" doctor that he returned when he wanted the drug again.

> It was the only safe way I could get a set of works. If I, a drug counselor, went out on a street corner and asked somebody for a set of works, the news would get back to Blue Hills before I arrived at my job the next morning. It would be as quick as if the message went by drumbeat.

He went to the doctor with "back pain." He was suffering a different kind of pain from problems he was having with his job and with the woman he lived with, problems that (as he realized in retrospect) had been building up for six months to a year. A week before he finally asked for the Dilaudid, Don took a box of 15-gauge hypodermic needles from the doctor's drug cabinet.

> So there I was, sitting in a motel room watching myself pump in four or five sixteenths of Dilaudid at a time. I was on my way back into addiction, and I was just watching it happen. And perhaps, if I'd been working in some other field, I might have continued. I still felt the strong pull of that magic I had found early in life that straightened me out and let me go about my business. And it's easy enough to get up in the morning, shoot two Dilaudids, and go to work and function without anybody being the wiser. I mean, in countries where it is legal, people take opium or morphine all the time — no problem.
>
> But being in an exposed position, I was faced with a choice. I realized that if I continued down that road, I would lose everything I had built up for myself since I came in off the street. I would lose people, relationships, my work — all the

> things I had come to value. I was very much afraid to lose those things, especially when I saw that the drug that used to take away all my pain wasn't doing it anymore. The thing that seven or eight years before had been my life no longer made me happy.

Don clearly cared enough about his new life to pull himself up out of the pit he had fallen into. Taking what he characterized as the "humiliating" step of going into a facility and detoxing, he then went to Blue Hills and voluntarily shared his experience with addict clients as well as staff members, thereby letting them express any anger they might feel toward him.

During his three-month suspension he came to live with Lee, just as Jerry was to do a year or so later when his home burned down. For Don it was a period of reflection reminiscent of his early days as a methadone patient.

> Again I had the chance to get away and evaluate my situation, my values, my choices. Again I found myself with time on my hands, time to think, to ask myself what made me happy and what I wanted to achieve. I asked myself whether I would be able to work at Blue Hills after the way I'd exposed myself there.
>
> At this time Lee, Jerry, the woman I'd been living with, and a few other people asserted their love and concern. Nobody lectured me; they simply made clear that it was important to them that I hold on to what made me happy. For the first time I was sure nobody was judging me on the basis of whether I was clean or not.

Lee's support manifested itself in numerous ways, one of which was by setting up meetings between Don and the administration at Blue Hills. Although Lee told Don that he wasn't sure if it was the wisest thing to confront the issue directly with people who might well have responded more punitively than they eventually did, he admired Don for his courage in doing so. As Don tells it:

> The only people who could really let me know were not the staff, but the people I counseled. Would they still listen to me? Could they get value from anything I gave them? Hearing what they had to say, I got a sense of when somebody was giving me a stroke to avoid confronting the real issue. "Listen," I would say, "you don't have to give me any bullshit. We've always talked honestly. You can tell me what you feel." And I found that some people couldn't accept what I had done, while with others I could work beyond it. At that point I reasserted myself, found some strength again. I made the decision to return to my job. I felt that I still had something to offer because by now I had gotten beyond working with drug groups. My groups were really people groups, working with people problems. We were beyond the issue of whether or not you got high; the issue was what you were doing with your life. At that level I felt I could still work with people, and was reaffirmed in that decision.

Looking back on these events three years later, Don said, "I believe I grew through the experience, because it taught me what was really important to me. It was important to see that people loved me; it enabled me to love myself a little more." In these words there was some truth, some lip service, and some real inner conflict, for they were spoken just months before Don hit a low point from which he would not be able to bounce back so quickly or easily.

***

Early in 1978 Don showed up in Lee's office looking "deathly ill." Deeply depressed, he complained both of physical ailments and of the effects of methadone in combination with a number of tranquilizers he was taking to ease the pain of what he felt were neurological problems. Lee, who had not seen Don for months, believed that his physical symptoms should be checked out first. He had Don admitted to a general hospital under the care of a physician and a psychiatrist. After giving Don every diagnostic test imaginable, the doctors found no physical basis for his complaints. What they did find was withdrawal from Valium and a variety of other tranquilizers and barbiturates (though apparently not narcotics). They found a lot of psychological pain, both resulting from and contributing to his drug use. Don then left the hospital "against medical advice."

As a result of his second "slip," Don was fired from his job at Blue Hills (although for some time he continued to receive partial payment as a form of insurance). Weeks earlier the chief counselor had said to him, "What's going on with you, Don? You look like you're stoned." Don had replied, "Oh, it's just from the medication." In Don's view, most of the people at Blue Hills did not show much commitment to him in his time of trouble.

> There were a few individuals who cared more about me as a person than about being upgraded. The rest had the attitude that "Don's job is on the line — I'd better stay clear of him." I spent all those years working side by side with people, and then they ran for cover and let me go down the tubes.

At the same time, he recognizes that he didn't make it easy for them to help him. During this period he also stayed completely out of touch with Lee.

Looking back, Don is now able to shed some light on how he was feeling when he began to act so unstably.

> It's like when somebody comes into a group and drops a few bombshells, and everybody thinks, "Wow — heavy revelations!" but then it turns out that he's been saying these things for years and that something else is bothering him. That's how it

> was with me. As an addict and later as a counselor I had been good with words, good at mesmerizing people. I shared things I was comfortable with, but I covered up the real pain. I didn't look in the mirror because I didn't want to see the reality there.
>
> By 1978 the shell game I had been running was finished. I knew that I was on a dead end street. I had used the counseling job, the fact that I had some skills, to paper over the fear, the rage, the depression, the paranoia. But now the job was no longer working for me, and all the feelings I had bottled up were coming to the surface. All the artificial supports were stripped away, and I was nakedly exposed as the person I was. By the time I left Blue Hills I was completely paralyzed and fearful of the future. What was the fear? What was the pain? It's not an easy question to answer in a few words. Mainly, I don't think I ever really felt adequate as a person. When it came to dealing with things on the natural (i.e., not on drugs), and even not on the natural, I was like a frightened child curled up in the corner.

In ways he cannot precisely pinpoint, Don's collapse was tied up with an intense relationship with a woman.

> At this time I had met someone who seemed to be able to give me more love, more of herself than anyone ever had. But I could not reciprocate. I clung to her to the point where it became disastrous for both of us. I can remember nights with her when all I did was cry over what I felt I couldn't stop, couldn't do anything about. I was on a road with no end.

After leaving the hospital Don vanished for several months. He went from one motel room to another, "isolating myself, knocking myself out with drugs."

> By then I didn't have any more relationships. I couldn't touch anyone, couldn't relate to women. My anxiety was so great that I only wanted to pass out in motel rooms. It was the worst period in my life. Strangely, though, it was also one of the most interesting, because now there was no more hiding from myself.

He "crashed" at a private psychiatric hospital. Lee will never forget what he saw when he visited him there.

> It was bizarre. There he was, lying on a cot in the main room of this place, hardly able to lift up his head. He was a wreck. He became more and more psychotic, more and more paranoid. He kept repeating that visitors to the hospital were really coming in to check up on him, that people were going to take him away, that he couldn't breathe and was going to die. And I thought maybe he really was going to die. In his fear of living without chemicals he appeared to be working himself up to die.

In his own account of this hospitalization, Don alternates between criticizing yet another insensitive institution and relating honestly the dire state he was in at the time.

> The counselors there were used to dealing with helpless people. When I came in and asked questions, they saw me as a threat to their power. They saw me as a slick dope fiend trying to manipulate them. Therefore they took away all the drugs and took me right off my feet. That was how Lee found me. Not only couldn't I get up off my back, but after awhile I even stopped talking. For weeks I didn't speak. Why should I speak

> when I had said it all? All the words I had used in the past had only brought me to that point. Somehow I wasn't communicating my needs, and people weren't listening anyway.
>
> I felt that people could see right through me; I could see through myself. Nothing was real. Yes, I believed that I was going to die. It was so easy to say, "Make the arrangements for my funeral." I didn't want to go out in the world again.

Was Don hitting a "bottom" he had never reached before? Was he facing death, as Lee had, so that he could rise again and face life? Or was this just another histrionic copout? Don sees it both ways, and subsequent events leave room for either interpretation.

When Don left the hospital, he was, in his own words, "a dishrag." For a while he lived at Lee's house, where he had all his everyday physical needs taken care of and was welcome to stay as long as he wanted. Lee and his family refused to hold his hand or play along with his helpless image. They made every effort to deal with him on an honest basis, just as they would with anyone else. Yet it wasn't always so easy, as Lee recalls.

> Sometimes he would show up for dinner so stoned that he couldn't carry on a conversation. My wife or my daughter would ask me when I was going to confront him about it. But I was hoping, fantasizing, that maybe this time would be different — so much so that I got into the same denial as Don. I would say, "Listen, I think he's just tired." And Pam and Leslie would say, "He's more than tired. He's really stoned." All my expertise was out the window. Lee, the famed counselor, was most ineffective. I felt funny being in that position with Don because I'm not his counselor. I can't be. I love him as a friend, as family.

While he was staying with Lee Don made big plans. Having nothing to do during the day, he announced that he was going to A.A. meetings. Great idea, said Lee. He didn't go. He talked for hours about fishing, but he never picked up a fishing pole. He said that he wanted to get into a rehabilitation program, but not in Connecticut, where he would be embarrassed to be a patient again after being a counselor. Lee obligingly made arrangements with a couple of programs in neighboring states. Don never showed up at either one.

Again he disappeared. Obsessed with his fears, looking for answers on a map, he ran to New York, to Boston. "I just couldn't sit down and relax," he reflects. "I couldn't stop and say, 'You know, I'm going to be okay. I'm aware of these things, and that in itself is a big step.'"

Returning to Hartford, Don lived on and off with his mother, who has always been willing to take care of him. Like most mothers, and like Lee, she would prefer to believe that "this time things will be different." Lee believed it enough to serve as a reference for Don in a financial matter which required an investment on someone else's part. When Don failed to fulfill his side of the agreement, Lee first tried to get in touch by phone, then wrote Don a note telling him that he was really disappointed in him. He reminded Don that there were many people who were trying to reach out to him and who would feel better if he would just keep in touch and let him know how he was doing, so that they wouldn't just be getting emergency calls from him.

Until recently Don remained incommunicado much of the time. At forty he did not have the ambition to live the street life, a life that can wear down a much younger man. Instead, as Lee put it, "He checked in for his methadone, made a buck here and there, and kept to himself in a small room."

***

For about ten years, with one lapse, Don thought he had surrendered illicit drug use. Then, when his life became less pleasant, he found out that his surrender was conditional. Along with the job burnout discussed in the previous chapter, his life was made less pleasant by problems with women. As he says, "I've always been frightened of relationships. If I can control a relationship, I can get by. But I'm so frightened that even my perceptions of women are distorted."

It wasn't that Don was unable to attract women. Quite the contrary. He is friendly, personable, witty, and speaks knowledgeably about many subjects. He is easy to like. Nor was it that he couldn't maintain a close, long-term relationship. For several years he lived with a woman who was a source of considerable support for him. Although he did not make a formal commitment of fidelity by marrying this woman, he actually lived out that commitment better than Lee and Jerry have sometimes done. Lee believes that Don's capacity for loyalty to a woman came from the intimacy and trust he always had with his mother. "He loves his mother and she loves him," says Lee, "and that's something Jerry and I never felt when we were young." With that love, however, came guilt. Don felt that he should reciprocate the sacrifices his mother made for him. With this background, on those occasions when he had the opportunity and the desire to be unfaithful to his girlfriend, Don was not likely to have an easy time of it.

Each time Don went back to using drugs, he began by having an affair outside his primary relationship. He may have been uncomfortable having sex with an unfamiliar woman without drugs. He certainly was uncomfortable cheating on his girlfriend. "His pattern is very consistent," Lee comments. "When he starts going out with women on other than a committed basis, he starts getting very nervous. And when he starts getting very nervous, he has to have something to kill the pain." That is where his conditional surrender comes in. There is still a little voice in Don's head that says that drugs can be an alternative when he feels he is under stress. By his own account, Don's current troubles began when he decided to let himself smoke "just one joint" each afternoon with a woman he was seeing.

Lee and Jerry obviously are not moralistic about sexual infidelity. If a person can be comfortable while venturing outside an exclusive love relationship, they say, then it won't be a problem as far as recovery is concerned. The issue is not whether Don was operating outside of other people's or society's values. If Don wanted to violate his commitment and not feel guilty about it, then he was in conflict with his own values. And as Jon Weinberg has noted, it is only natural for a person who has previously resolved value conflicts by means of an addiction to look for the same solution again.

***

Each answer only leads to another question. Given that Don had problems and frustrations, as anyone does, what made him finally turn back to drugs as a way of coping with them? And what made him compound his problems by standing still while the world kept going? In staying at Blue Hills Don let himself get stuck at an early plateau of growth. In his words, "I tried to stop the clock. Although I did broaden my interests outside the job, I never looked beyond the job and asked, 'Where do I want to go?' I put it off." When conditions changed and new choices were required, he did not have the options. He had not prepared himself to move to a higher plateau. As the plateau he had reached collapsed under him, he had nowhere to go but down.

Back in 1970 Don's recovery may well have looked as solid as Lee's or Jerry's. In retrospect, though, his surrender of illegal narcotics appears to have had a situational quality, like Lee's "controlled drinking." Don gave up heroin and Dilaudid in return for methadone and a state job. He made an agreement that, as long as he had those compensations, he would stay clean and work conscientiously at Blue Hills — an agreement which he kept. On the early tapes many of Don's remarks sound like verbatim echoes of Lee's — celebrating the choice of "people" and "love" over drugs, rhapsodizing over sunrises and sunsets and holidays without drugs, saying that "every day clean has been better than any day "high," and so forth. By repeating sayings like these at A.A. or at Blue Hills, Lee and others have learned to live out the sentiments they express. It made sense for Don to model himself after Lee, but he never grew into the role. He never came to feel the slogans inwardly or put them into action as Lee did. His commitment to grow was not reinforced by performance.

This is not to say that he was dissembling. He really wanted to learn these positive sentiments, and he may have believed that he was learning them. But he seems never to have gotten beyond the dilemma that, as a counselor, he observed in his clients.

> I get frustrated when somebody in our program gets a job where he makes perhaps just enough to get off welfare. Then he walks through a shopping mall and sees stereos, TVs, fur coats flying out at him. These are the rewards society offers this guy for taking the "right" path, and he wants them right away. He wants *something* in return for giving up the other thing.

Lee has said that he couldn't give up something that made him feel "good" until he found something else that made him feel better. But the "something" he was referring to was not stereos, TVs, and fur coats, but the unconditional love and support that enabled him to accept himself and to enlarge himself. If one demands immediate material rewards for giving up drugs, then one's surrender is conditional.

To hear him speak, one would gather that Don has gained a perspective on the quest for material gratifications.

> The next step in finding out about reality is when you *do* get the rewards. Then you learn that they're not what you imagined when you were just dreaming about them. I remember standing on a street corner one winter day, waiting for the cop man. I was freezing there, and along came a guy in a sports car with skis on the back and a good-looking blonde nestled up beside him. What I would have given to change places with that man. What I later found out, after I became the guy behind the wheel, was that he probably broke his leg on the slopes, saw the girl go off with somebody else, and had his car repossessed three weeks later.

Maybe Don learned this lesson too late (in his own eyes) to make up for the years he spent trying to get the car and the skis and the woman. Maybe he still hasn't learned it. As Lee and Jerry see him, Don is still the guy on the street corner dreaming, not the disillusioned guy behind the wheel.

When Lee and Jerry talk about further growth during recovery, they talk not only about plays and concerts and camping trips, but about schooling and relationships — about facing and mastering challenges. When Don talks about growth he talks about photography. Photography has meant a lot to Don. He is very good at it, and it undoubtedly gave him some self-respect and contentment during his early recovery. But he put a lot of his modest salary into getting the best camera equipment, and a lot of his time into using it, when he might have put some money and time into strengthening himself and increasing his opportunities.

While Lee was still working at Blue Hills, Don would say to him, "Hey, have you seen the new 280-Z? You should get yourself one!" This was when lee was getting himself an education in the evenings while his wife worked. Lee and Jerry sacrificed a few years of long hours and financial hardship to put themselves in line for greater success later. They saw far enough into the future to be able to postpone gratifications. Don made a different choice. He wanted the externals, and he wanted them right away. He wanted the Nikon camera, the Bill Blass clothes. Don is the only person Lee has ever known who reads *Gentleman's Quarterly.*

No one was more thrilled than Don when Jerry earned his bachelor's degree. He couldn't stop telling Lee what a great accomplishment it was. As for doing it himself, he thought that was a great idea, too. Lee's friend and colleague Linda Roberts got Don a tutor who would have "walked him through" his high school equivalency exam, but he didn't stick with it. Jerry took him by the hand, registered him for a course in Basic Studies at the University of Connecticut, and ended up forfeiting the $10 registration fee when Don never came back. Lee signed him up for a course at the Hartford Graduate Center and sat with him through the first session. Lee waited for Don to show up for the second session, but it was like waiting for Godot. "Godot," in fact, was what Don came to be called affectionately by his friends.

Don liked the thought of taking these courses, but then a movie would come to town, or there woud be an automobile rally in the area, or he wouldn't want to miss something on television. Don did not have the achievement-oriented background that Jerry and Lee did. Even as a child Jerry had to work for everything he got. Lee learned to follow in his father's productive path even if he didn't enjoy it. Those experiences shaped the two men's careers in addiction and their later careers as helping professionals. Jerry and Lee have always been enterprising businessmen. While Jerry was a big-time operator in the dope world, Don was content to remain a user. In later years, in order to establish themselves professionally, Lee and Jerry put in 18-hour days on the road doing workshops where they barely made their expenses. Don would not have understood what they were doing it for. When he was growing up he did not have models of that kind of effort. As Jerry puts it,

> In the last twenty years there have been three major league baseball players who never played in the minors. Speaking metaphorically, I am not among them. My apprenticeship in the minor leagues was long and hot. Don wanted to go right to the major leagues. The tragic thing about it is that he ended up staying in the minors.

Still, Don didn't have to have Lee's or Jerry's entrepreneuria energy to get out of the rut in which he was trapped. If he had gone to school and obtained some credentials he could have become a couseling administrator, enjoying professional status along with the security of state employment, as one of his and Jerry's former colleagues at Blue Hills has done. He didn't even have to go to school; nor did he have to stay in the counseling field. He could have made it as a photographer. At the suggestion of an acquaintance Don submitted some of his photographs to the public television station in Hartford, which had a job opening for a photographer. Despite Don's lack of formal training, the station management took one look at his work and said, "Get this person down here. We want him." But they were waiting for Godot. So was a New Jersey editor who left several long-distance phone messages for Don at Lee's house (where he was then staying) indicating that he wanted to publish a few of his photos.

Lee shakes his head when he thinks of all those missed opportunities. "God, so many times, so many times," he says sadly. Don has broken every commitment requiring real personal effort — with schools and tutors, with a "no-BS shrink" he saw a few times, with an educated woman whose expectations he feared he couldn't meet.

Even with his love of pleasure, even with his lack of ambition, the big hurdle for Don is pain. He is afraid of the unknown, afraid to risk himself. He will not subject himself to what he perceives as the pressure of other people's expectations. Not only will he not risk having his performance evaluated in school; he also will not risk having his performance evaluated as a photographer. He will not put himself in a situation where people expect him to produce and are not concerned about his feelings.As much as he loves photography, as good as he is at it, he has not put himself on the line to make it his life's work.

Someone once said of Don, "He's afraid of failure, and he's afraid of success." Indeed, he is afraid of all the little failures that go along with success. He probably isn't sure that he could face having his employer tell him that one photograph out of a whole project isn't quite right. This is how Lee pictures Don's thought processes:

> Whenever Don thinks about really doing something, really making a move, he must run a very fast tape in his head, like a speeded-up movie. It starts from failure, goes to success, shows the pain that comes with success, and goes back to failure — all in about thirty-seconds. It's like when you're thinking about going out on a date with someone, and you start tripping out on all the things you don't like about her and all the

> things she might not like about you. Before you know it you've got children and then grandchildren, and she's a big nuisance when she gets old, and you say, "The heck with it, I'm not going out with her." And all this time you haven't even left your room. That's how I see Don. He just trips out on all the fantasies of the bad things that could happen to him.

Albert Ellis says, "There is no gain without pain." Don knows it, wishes it weren't so, and chooses to live inside his wishes.

***

Don admits that he cannot cope with pain and fear in a drug-free state. "I used to be a heroin addict," he says. "Now I'm a methadone addict." Yet Don has been on methadone when he passed up the educational and job opportunities his friends arranged for him. What has stopped him from acting even *with* the support of the drug?

Don's answer is that he has found it to be just as debilitating to be a methadone "patient" as to do without the drug. In the first place, his having to check in at the methadone clinic every morning rules out the flexible schedule required of a professional photographer. "How can I commit myself to being where I'm needed when I'm needed," he asks, "when I'm tied down like this?" In addition, Don regards the clinic procedure itself as degrading. In his view, urine tests and embarrassing questions are used to keep clients "off balance," to keep them "in their place." These "subliminal controls," he believes, have two functions. One is to keep the clinic running in an orderly manner. "I feel," says Don, "as if I'm in a Skinner box where they run me in one door and out the other like an experimental rat." The second purpose is more sinister. Methadone maintenance is a big business, supported by government money. According to Don, it would not be in the interest of the program to build up an addict's strength so that he could live without methadone, since the program is funded according to the number of addicts it serves.

Whether or not there is any truth to these allegations, the very fact that Don must go to the clinic every day for methadone reminds him constantly of his own insufficiency. This probably would be the case even if the drug were to be dispensed in an ideally humane manner. As Don tells it,

> Methadone had gotten to be like heroin: I can't function without it, and I can't function with it. After about six or eight years I realized that as long as I was on methadone and wasn't in any serious therapy, I wasn't going anywhere. "Maybe something will change," I would say to myself, but I wasn't about to do anything. I was waiting for Godot. I don't care what trappings, what Bill Blass jacket I had, I was still a methadone addict, and I was always aware of it. It interfered with any relationship I had, just as it interfered with my job. What an irony — here I was sitting in groups counseling people when I myself couldn't get off methadone. I think you could go out and get a Ph.D., but if you're still going through that clinic, you'll feel like shit.

Don is saying here that the addiction cycle is still operating for him, in that his guilt about being drug-dependent reduces his self-esteem, which in turn keeps him drug-dependent. Having to take methadone prevents him from developing the satisfactions and accomplishments in life that would give him the strength to give up the methadone. It is a telling indictment of methadone maintenance as a long-term treatment for heroin addicts. As Don has learned, methadone is a subsititute addiction that reinforces the underlying pattern of chemical dependency. It should be seen, he now believes, only as a "temporary necessity" for those addicts who need it.

> Methadone is a lifesaver when you're out on the street. When I was just coming in out of the cold, it was easy to compromise by accepting the urinalyses, the humiliations and degradations that went with methadone. But I've been around

> long enough to see that it only works up to a point. I've seen more than one guy who was successful on the program for maybe ten years, but then his marriage, say, would break up. His wife would say, "What's this shit? Five years ago, okay, but this is ten years now!"

Don regards himself and others as having "sold out" for methadone plus a job as a counselor. As long as he was being protected from the hazards of the street life and given legitimate employment, he "closed his eyes" to the faults of the treatment program and did not sufficiently extend himself ("make waves") on behalf of the addicts he served. Now he feels free to look at the larger picture. The major shortcoming that he sees in many drug treatment programs is that they are oriented to the past and present, but not the future. They give a diagnosis (addiction) and a treatment (methadone), but what about the prognosis? An addict is not *only* an addict, but also a person with the capacity to be educated and to work productively. In order to realize that potential, Don believes that addicts coming into treatment should be given intensive therapy with the goal of helping them progress beyond the methadone maintenance within five years. It hurts him to see people come into a program at the age of 18 and still be in the same place psychologically five years later. He also advocates freeing methadone patients who show a serious interest in self-development from the daily clinic routine. This could be done by authorizing therapists to prescribe a month's supply of methadone, under the same regulations that control the abuse of other prescription drugs. With this freedom, Don maintains, he himself could still have a chance to become the person he wants to be.

Don is now working with other methadone patients to present this point of view forcefully to the relevant public agencies. The opportunity to engage in political organizing in support of a cause he believes in has given him renewed energy and purpose. No longer does he sit in a room all day. He is, in fact, negotiating with a prospective partner to go into business as a photographer. It is a hopeful moment in his life.

***

Lee and Jerry share a certain pragmatic quality, an attentiveness to changes in the environment. It is more evident in Jerry, who always has lived by his wits and has made many compromises in order to survive. Jerry is reminiscent of the Roman Emperor Claudius in Robert Graves' *I, Claudius,* whose life was one long series of survival acts, the last one being (when he had no other choice) to let himself be made emperor. Jerry cleaned up his act when he found that he could survive better by playing the rehabilitation game than the addiction game. Lee, with his histrionic suicide attempts, lived with apparent abandon. Yet a man who smashed up several cars and walked away unscathed, a man who came out of twenty years of hard drinking and pill-popping physically and mentally intact, must have had a strong self-preserving tendency somewhere within him. After telling himself for twenty years that giving up the fight would mean death, he saw that he had reached a point where going on with the fight would mean death. Like Jerry, he knew he was licked. Both of them knew when they had hit bottom.

Don, too, is preoccupied with survival. Up to now, though, he has survived by leaning on props that have cushioned the "bottom" for him. These props include methadone as well as a protective family, friends, and co-workers. Finally, he has been able to fall back on his "heart problems," "nerve disorders," and "mental breakdowns." It is intriguing to look at Don's recent psychotic episode in the light of his staged catatonic act almost twenty years earlier. The play-acting has come closer to home. It has become harder for Don to sort out what is real from what is not. Yet he still finds ways to "bug out" of what to him is unpleasant or uncomfortable, including much of what we think of as normal life.

On the other hand, it has been three years since his breakdown, and he appears to be moving away from that way of coping. Perhaps Don is only now hitting bottom. Perhaps his recent miseries have finally demonstrated to him that the pain of taking some steps in another direction cannot be any worse than the pain of going on as he has been.

Meanwhile, Lee has made clear to Don that he is still welcome, always welcome. He has told him, "It's okay. I'm not your counselor. If you want to stay in that other life, you don't have to stay away from me. I'm still here for you. We can still be friends. I love you."

***

Don's inability thus far to make his recovery stick illuminates and is illuminated by Lee's and Jerry's successful recoveries. All Don had to lose by going back to drugs was a deteriorating situation as a counselor at Blue Hills. Lee and Jerry would stand to lose a lot more — well-paying professional careers, satisfying personal relationships, the respect of many people to whose lives they have contributed, and (most important) a self-respect and integrity that make the whole question of relapse academic. Their identities are predicated on their recovery. Their life structures reinforce them in their renunciation of addiction. If they returned to drug or alcohol abuse, they would risk having those structures collapse around them. It is, of course, highly unlikely that they would do this. It is highly unlikely that they would even contemplate it.

Jerry, who never needed methadone, says flatly that it is absurd to think that he could ever use drugs again. Lee sticks to the A.A. motto, "One day at a time," and speaks of "eternal vigilance." But he adds:

> Well, in my case I don't really mean vigilance about drugs and alcohol. I don't seriously think they'll ever again be a problem for me. It's the "thinking" that can still be a problem. The issue isn't really the chemicals; it's the things that make for a reasonable or unreasonable lifestyle. So it's eternal vigilance about living that I'm talking about. It's as important for someone who has never had a problem with drugs or alcohol as it is for me.
>
> As I enter my fiftieth year I continue to search for the closeness, the connection, the affection, the unquestioning acceptance. I feel safer, but

> not completely safe. The wounds of the past, the pain — they come alive when least expected. But now it is not with alcohol or drugs that I will fight these dragons, but with myself. Some days I do better than others. As I reach mid-century I feel my limits and rage against them. Why can't I ever feel as though I have enough? More accomplishments . . . more work . . . the phantom "Great Love."
>
> I want it all.
>
> My self-doubt, dissatisfaction, moodiness, "if onlys" do battle with me. They continue and I continue. Sometimes I exchange one form of unhappiness for another, but more often I win.
>
> I try not to look backward, but there is the longing, the bitterness, the feeling, thoughts, fears, doubts. At times they make me an "infatuation junkie." I have lived with despair, with isolation as bad company, with emotional starvation and emotional bankruptcy. I have known what "nothing" means. Yet I have learned the pleasures of risking, touching, compassion, non-judgmental love, joy, and enthusiasm, and I will opt for those prizes each time. I have risked the transparency and found a pleasure that is often spiritual. No longer self-absorbed at all times with that emptiness, that craving for approval, I believe that, as Schweitzer put it, human encounters rekindle the inner light, and that, as Mother Theresa tells us, the mistakes of kindness and compassion are so much more fruitful than all that the search for magic cures can ever reveal.

Lee's lifestyle is expansive and inspirational. He thrives on exchange. Every person he meets, every book he reads, every conversation he has, every A.A. meeting he attends becomes a bit of vital energy for the fund of love and support in which he now deposits far more than he withdraws. As he says at the conclusion of *Consider the Alternative,* "What's mine is mine — and yours, too." His recovery has been steeped in rhetoric — the mystical, celebratory rhetoric of a religious conversion. Jerry, skeptical pragmatist to the end, acknowledges a great deal of continuity in his life. He has been known to say things like, "I'm still the same person I was when I was out on the street dealing — just doing different things." Then, taking in his cozy basement study with a sweep of his arm, he adds, "This is better." That he and Lee are both right — about themselves and each other — shows the rare complexity of the struggle they have been through.

references

Introduction

1. Peele, Stanton; with Brodsky, Archie. *Love and Addiction.* New York: Taplinger, 1975; New American Library, 1976.
2. Peele, Stanton. "Redefining Addiction I. Making Addiction a Scientifically and Socially Useful Concept." *International Journal of Health Services,* 1977, *7,* 103-124. "Addiction: The Analgesic Experience." *Human Nature,* September 1978, 61-67. "Redefining Addiction II. The Meaning of Addiction in Our Lives." *Journal of Psychedelic Drugs,* 1979, *11,* 289-297.
3. Silverstein, Lee M.; with Brett, Jon; Roberts, Linda. *Consider the Alternative.* Minneapolis: CompCare Publications, 1977.
4. Edelwich, Jerry; with Brodsky, Archie. *Burn-out: Stages of Disillusionment in the Helping Professions.* New York: Human Sciences Press, 1980.

Chapter 1

1. Chein, Isidor. "Psychological Functions of Drug Use." In Steinberg, Hannah (ed.), *Scientific Basis of Drug Dependence.* London: J. & A. Churchill, 1969, pp. 13-30.
2. Chein, Isidor; Gerard, Donald L.; Lee, Robert S.; Rosenfeld, Eva. *The Road to H.* New York: Basic Books, 1964.
3. Horney, Karen. *Neurosis and Human Growth.* New York: Norton, 1950.

Chapter 2

1. Luce, John. "End of the Road: A Case Study." In Smith, David E.; Gay, George R. (eds.), *"It's So Good, Don't Even Try It Once": Heroin in Perspective.* Englewood Cliffs, N.J.; Prentice-Hall, 1972, pp. 143-147.
2. Winick, Charles. "Maturing Out of Narcotic Addiction." *Bulletin on Narcotics,* 1962, *14,* 1-7.
3. McClelland, David C.; Davis, William N.; Kalin, Rudolf; Wanner, Eric. *The Drinking Man.* New York: Free Press, 1972.
4. Kolb, Lawrence. *Drug Addiction: A Medical Problem.* Springfield, Ill.; Charles C Thomas, 1962.

Chapter 3

1. Kaplan, Eugene H.; Wieder, Herbert. *Drugs Don't Take People; People Take Drugs.* Secaucus, N.J.: Lyle Stuart, 1974.
2. Robins, Lee N.; Davis, D.H.; Goodwin, D.W. "Drug Use by U.S. Army Enlisted Men in Vietnam: A Follow-up on Their Return Home." *American Journal of Epidemiology* 1974, *99,* 235-249.
3. Zinberg, Norman E.; Robertson, John A. *Drugs and the Public.* New York: Simon & Schuster, 1972.
4. Zinberg, Norman E. "The Search for Rational Approaches to Heroin Use." In Peter G. Bourne (ed.), *Addiction.* New York: Academic Press, 1974.
5. LeFlore, Ron; Hawkins, J. "Stealing Was My Specialty." *Sports Illustrated,* February 6, 1978, pp. 62-74.
6. Winick, Charles. "Physician Narcotic Addicts." *Social Problems,* 1961, *9,* 174-186.

Chapter 4

1. Pet, Donald. "Socio-cultural Implications of Drug Abuse." In *Drug Abuse: A Course for Educators.* A report of the Butler University Drug Abuse Institute, Indianapolis, Ind. Cf. Alksne, Harold; Lieberman, Louis; Brill, Leon. "A Conceptual Model of the Life Cycle of Addiction." *International Journal of the Addictions,* 1967, *2,* 221-240.
2. Preble, Edward; Casey, John J., Jr. "Taking Care of Business: The Heroin User's Life on the Street." In Smith & Gay, op. cit, pp. 97-118.
3. Kaplan & Wieder, op. cit.

Chapter 6

1. Tiebout, Harry M. *The Act of Surrender in the Therapeutic Process,* pp. 9-10. Distributed by the National Council on Alcoholism, Inc., New York.
2. Powell, John. *The Secret of Staying in Love.* Niles, Ill.: Argus Communications, 1974. *Fully Human, Fully Alive.* Niles, Ill.: Argus Communications, 1976.

Chapter 7

1. Glasser, William. *Reality Therapy.* New York: Harper & Row, 1965; Perennial Library, 1975, p. 15.
2. Ellis, Albert; Harper, Robert A. *A New Guide to Rational Living,* N. Hollywood, Cal.: Wilshire Book Co., 1975.
3. Simon, Sidney B.; Howe, Leland W.; Kirschenbaum, Howard. *Values Clarification.* New York: Hart, 1972.

Chapter 8

1. Edelwich with Brodsky, op. cit.
2. Weinberg, Jon R. *Sex and Recovery.* Minneapolis: Recovery Press, 1977.

Chapter 9

1. Malcolm, Andrew I. *The Craving for the High.* Markham, Ontario: Simon & Schuster, 1975.